NATURAL BUILDING
A Guide to Materials and Techniques

NATURAL BUILDING
A Guide to Materials and Techniques

Tom Woolley

THE CROWOOD PRESS

First published in 2006 by
The Crowood Press Ltd
Ramsbury, Marlborough
Wiltshire SN8 2HR

www.crowood.com

British Library Cataloguing-in-Publication Data
A catalogue record for this book is available from the British Library.

ISBN 1 86126 841 6
EAN 978 1 86126 841 9

Disclaimer
The author and the publisher do not accept responsibility, nor liability, in any manner
whatsoever for any error or omission, nor any loss, damage, injury, or adverse outcome of any
kind incurred as a result of the use of the information contained in this book, or reliance upon
it. Readers are advised to seek specific professional advice relating to their particular house,
construction, project and circumstances before embarking on any building work.

Line drawings by Melissa Hamilton.
Photographs by Tom Woolley, unless otherwise stated.

Front cover: The workshop/office of Sally Ruel Architect and Quercus Rural Building Design,
Borders, Scotland.
Back cover: (top left) Loch Lomond Visitor Centre, Rowardennan, built with cob walls by
Rebecca Little, Architects Simpson and Brown; (top right) timber-roofed building at the top
of the water-balanced railway at the Centre for Alternative Technology, Machynlleth,
Architects Pat Borer and David Lea; (bottom right) internal hemp lime wall in a Suffolk
Housing Society house in Haverhill, Modece Architects.
Frontispiece: Kitchen and restaurant at the Kindersley Centre, Berkshire. The staircase wraps
around a bread oven.

Typeset by Jean Cussons Typesetting, Diss, Norfolk

Printed and bound in Malaysia by the Alden Group

Contents

Foreword

Natural Building could easily be taken as another explanation of what sustainable development really means. Buildings are the most visible and tangible sign of economic development anywhere in the world: 'natural' speaks for itself, indicating the use of materials and processes that are compatible with the workings of the natural world. The fact that so few buildings emerging in our midst could in any way be described as 'natural' serves as a powerful reminder of just how unsustainable most economic development still is.

But the optimist in me tells me that things are at last changing. What was once the exclusive preserve of a bunch of starry-eyed aficionados of sustainable development is now being 'mainstreamed' across all walks of life. Governments declare allegiance to the principles of sustainable development at every available opportunity; big business struggles to make sense of the practice of it. The threat of traumatic climate change and the impacts of collapsing eco-systems across the world have, at long last, galvanized the world's elites into some kind of muddled response – as if they had suddenly woken up to the truth first uttered by E.F. Schumacher more than thirty years ago: 'Modern man still talks of the battle with Nature, forgetting that if he ever won the battle, he would find himself on the losing side'.

That's the big picture within which Tom Woolley's *Natural Building* needs to be set. As he says, most of those engaged in natural building today are not just 'ahead of their time', but 'pioneers in a hostile land'. The mainstream construction industry remains for the most part deeply conservative, weighted down by inflexible rulebooks and 'more than my life's worth'

mindsets. And it remains largely disconnected from the natural world, or any understanding of how natural systems actually work.

The author takes the fight to them robustly but pragmatically – the simple truth of it is that it's just very difficult persuading architects, planners and all the different professionals involved in the building business to fling off their shackles. And just to be even-handed about it, he's also got little time for the new army of 'envirocrats', who he sees as part of the problem rather than part of the solution.

I welcome that kind of controversy. There are very different views, for instance, on what is described today as 'micro-generation' – the use of small-scale renewable and sustainable energy technologies to reduce overall energy consumption and make it more sustainable. For me, this is a revolution in waiting – and I don't think we'll be waiting much longer either!

But we need to think carefully about how to make that 'distributed energy revolution' compatible with natural building. It's important that people start to think much more systematically about the whole of the construction supply chain, about where building materials come from, about how much embodied energy they contain, about the amount of waste they cause to be generated, and so on.

Natural building is no more uncontroversial a topic than sustainable development itself – which may well explain why I had such a good time immersing myself in this admirably instructive and uplifting work!

Jonathon Porritt

Acknowledgements

Many people have provided support, help and encouragement for this book. The most important of them are the many builders, architects, owners and occupants of buildings that feature in the book in pictures or in the text. Contacting people and asking whether I could visit their buildings and take photographs was a most heart-warming experience. Some drove me around to buildings I might never have found otherwise and others have gone out of their way to send me pictures or information. Almost everyone knew about at least one more project that I had not heard of, and in the end it was impossible to follow up all the leads. It was important for me to do as many visits as possible as this fired my enthusiasm for writing, but it also made me realize that there really is a natural building movement in the United Kingdom and Ireland. It is not just a question of a handful of quirky examples, but they are spread throughout the country.

Inspiration came from Christopher Day, Colin Ward, Walter Segal, Bruce and Sarah King, Rebecca Little, Tom Morton and Sam Kimmins, and the book could not have been written without the help of Professor Pete Walker, Dr Steve Goodhew, Neil May, Andy Warren, Nick Grant, Melissa Hamilton, Gary Newman and Ian Pritchett.

Thanks are also due to Patrick Waterfield, Geoff Smith, Jane Powell, Helen Ireland, Maddy Harland, Ben Law, Jimena Romero, Henry Thompson, Celia Spouncer, John Hobson, Chris Tweed, Alison Pooley, Mark Alexander, Lucy Pedlar, Cindy Harris, David Lea, Joe Kennedy, Andy Horn, Simon Fairlie, Liz McIlhagger, Desmond Ng and many others too.

Most importantly, thanks are due to Oliver, Hannah and Rachel, for giving me the space in which to work on the book, and to my father Jim Woolley.

CHAPTER 1

Introduction

WHAT IS NATURAL BUILDING?

'The job of shaping the built environment comes with a responsibility beyond the wants of the paying client, and beyond our personal wants as well. May the wisdom that we bring to our practice include an understanding of the effects of our building designs and materials choices on all beings now alive and their descendants.' (Elizabeth and Adams)

The aim of this book is to introduce the reader to the ideas and practice of natural building and to demonstrate that it is something that is now established in the United Kingdom and Ireland. Natural building embraces a wide range of concepts both in theory and practice, but I hope that after reading the book the difference between natural building and conventional building will become clear.

The context for natural building is that of global warming, environmental disasters and increasing fuel prices. This means that societies have to take a fresh look at every aspect of life and to question whether the planet and people can continue down the present road. There is little doubt that conventional building construction uses a great deal of fossil fuel and scarce, non-renewable resources, whereas natural building offers a range of alternatives, which use much less energy and resources that cause much less environmental damage.

Most of the people who are attracted to natural building techniques share a concern to behave more responsibly towards the environment, but, as will become apparent, many of these are individuals trying to do something different on their own. There are also examples of organizations with bigger projects

embracing natural building ideas, and many projects are environmental or organic centres that have adopted natural building as a physical expression of their aims. In time, the mainstream construction industry will have to adopt natural building methods and materials, but environmental problems will have to become more pressing before this happens.

The other aspect of natural building is not informed by doom and gloom prophecies of environmental catastrophe, but because it is more attractive, creates more beautiful and harmonious buildings and generally makes its occupants feel better. Given the choice between a 'cheap' synthetic material, product or method of building and a natural one, a subjective decision for the natural option is made. There may be an awareness of the scientific and environmental reasons but not always an understanding of the technical detail. Intuition leads to the natural alternative.

In our modern technocratic society we do not trust our intuition enough and clever advertising and offers of quick-fix solutions can easily sway us. The building industry is very conservative and seems to believe that nothing will work or last unless it is full of toxic glues, chemicals and comes with three layers of plastic wrapping. The client for a building who wants to use natural materials and methods will get plenty of hostile advice that 'it will never work' or

OPPOSITE: The Cobtun house in Worcester; designed by Associated Architects, this award-winning house includes a cob wall and other environmental features. It has featured in architectural magazines, showing that ecological design is achieving recognition as modern architecture.

'we've never done it like that'. Some professionals will be unwilling to embark on what they see as untried and experimental techniques that are not covered by British Standards, Board of Agrément certificates, warranties and indemnity insurance.

Natural building is still at a pioneering stage and there is much work to be done to demonstrate that the methods and materials described here are going to be problem-free, will be durable and meet the regulations. There is a need for scientific research and changes in official regulations and standards. It is hoped that this book will contribute towards a recognition that natural building is the way forward and encourage more pioneers to try out the possibilities outlined below.

For some, natural building means incorporating only a few natural materials into buildings that are otherwise conventional in concept. The basic building may be full of concrete, aluminium, steel and plastic, but some natural materials are added to give a natural impression, or to suggest that sustainability criteria are being met. Sustainable building is bedevilled by *greenwash* and increasingly marketing campaigns try to persuade us that energy-guzzling, polluting materials and processes are good for the environment. Some of the examples illustrated here may not have gone all the way in embracing natural building principles, but much can still be learnt from the materials that have been used.

At the other end of the spectrum, there are people who are trying to create buildings that, in their totality, have a minimal impact on the environment by using natural and local materials for almost every aspect. This holistic approach to natural building can also involve compromise, pragmatic decisions and choices and it seems pointless to indulge in a moralistic debate about whether our approach is more zero-impact than that of someone else. On the other hand, it is important to be aware that the use of manufactured and imported materials does have an environmental penalty and that this is a decision to be made with care.

'KNITTED' ARCHITECTURE

Natural building is a difficult issue for many architects who have been educated in a culture that despises the aesthetics of what they see as 'twee' vernacular cottages. Modern architecture, they suggest, involves grand statements in steel, glass and concrete following the avant-garde of the day, whereas those architects who work in a modern vernacular idiom, using natural and sustainable materials, find it hard to win design awards and praise from the high priests of modern architectural taste. Many of the examples here will be dismissed as 'hairy' buildings, but they have been selected as demonstrating a method of building rather than on aesthetic grounds. Even though I am a professor of architecture, I disavow the sneering, judgemental attitude that so infects my profession and welcome the ability of ordinary people to express their own ideas and creativity through building. Often self-builders do not get it right and the ideal result is more likely to come from a creative partnership where an architect or designer listens to and works with the aspirations of his client rather than his imposing some preconceived aesthetic solution.

Like many others of my generation, I was influenced by Bernard Rudofsky's book *Architecture without Architects*, which made it acceptable to admire the beauty of buildings that had happened rather than had been designed. Other writers such as Stewart Brand and Christopher Alexander have challenged normal architectural assumptions, showing that the best buildings are timeless and are shaped by change and alteration by the people who use them. Often this results in a simple beauty and harmony, which is not contrived but comes from the good intentions of the people carrying out a project. Suffice it to say, that most natural buildings exhibit a range of characteristics from a 'wibbly-wobbly' crudeness or kitsch, to an innocent charm and even high sophistication.

HOW THE BOOK CAN BE USED

It is hoped that this book will be useful to both the professionals who are considering designing and specifying with natural building techniques and to the growing number of their clients, from public authorities to commercial businesses, who want a more sustainable solution to their needs. It should also be useful to environmentalists who want to extend their green activities into the buildings they use and build. Some of the examples here relate to environmental organizations that have tried to demonstrate best practice in the buildings that they occupy. On the other hand, it is shameful that many environmental bodies fail to make the connections and barely extend even to using low-energy light bulbs in their own premises, failing to set a good example to others. Finally, the work should be helpful to the growing band of well-informed self-builders and members of the public who are tired of waiting for government policies and want to live a greener lifestyle now. It is the demand from consumers for natural buildings, materials and products that will drive changes in the industry and force the government to changes policies and introduce the appropriate legislation. Unfortunately, most initiatives to tackle the environmental crisis are concentrated on generating renewable energy instead of using less energy. Reducing consumption and using materials and methods that need minimal manufacturing and transportation should be a much higher priority.

It is also a problem that many think that the best way to have greener buildings is to use high levels of toxic insulation products and install expensive pieces of equipment such as photovoltaic cells and heat pumps. The book does not deal with these technological fixes. Many natural builders and buildings use renewable energy when appropriate and affordable, but are primarily trying to develop a lower-impact outcome.

Most people have some ideas about greener and natural buildings, they may have seen straw-bale buildings on the television or a grass roof, but do not realize the many other facets of natural building and how it is possible to approach most aspects of building from this perspective. They may be surprised to find how many examples of natural buildings illustrate the book and how widespread and innovative they are, but these examples are only a small sample of the ones that were visited and photographed.

In many cases the location of buildings is not explicit because individual householders want their

The grid-shell roof building at the Institute of Life Sciences, Pishwanton, Scotland; architect Christopher Day and engineer David Tasker, two of the most influential pioneers of ecological design. (Photo: David Tasker)

privacy and do not want Sunday drivers turning up to look at their houses. On the other hand, some buildings are public and can be visited. There are also organizations and centres that run courses and it is advisable to go on a hands-on course if you are thinking of using some of these techniques. There are also a growing number of companies supplying natural materials and products from eco-builders, merchants or by mail. Some products can even be obtained from mainstream suppliers. Natural building is growing in popularity and this will make it more feasible. The most useful source for information about this is the Association of Environment Conscious Builders.

THE CHANGING NATURE OF MATERIALS

Another source of inspiration for natural building is that of traditional and vernacular architecture. Indeed, many will view some of the techniques here as 'turning the clock back'. However, humanity has always used natural materials to create shelter and many people in the world still rely on locally extracted and harvested materials. Obviously, if you are poor then you have to make do with whatever is to hand. Often this means recycling waste or scrap materials, or it can mean using grasses, turf, earth, clay or stone or even caves. This has led to a local character for buildings as well as having a low impact.

11

Industry and technology have developed thousands of new products for building and these have gradually replaced local traditional materials. Buildings are made from products supplied by builders merchants and they may be manufactured anywhere in the world and go through several forms of processing and transportation. Often as much is spent on marketing, packaging and transport as on the material itself, and now we have come to take for granted that these manufactured materials are readily available and that they are the best things to use when we build. Modern materials using glass, cement, concrete, aluminium, steel and plastics are essential parts of modern buildings and it would be hard to do without them. Increasingly builders look to produce buildings in ways that eliminate labour, craftsmanship and the 'wet trades' such as brick and block-laying and plastering since few tradesmen now have these skills and many young people do not want to go into the building industry. As a result, buildings depend more and more on new industrial materials and less on what appear to be wet, dirty, messy, traditional materials. Technological innovation is mostly driven by the profitability of builders and developers, and not the welfare of the occupants. This is often presented as a drive for greater efficiency and even sustainability, but a construction industry that is largely responsible for de-skilling is more concerned with cutting corners than the long-term quality of the buildings that are produced. The built environment is central to our economy, it affects all of us. However, the way in which it consumes natural resources means that it is one of the most significant contributors to global and local environmental problems. The way we use materials, the pollution emitted from building and manufacturing and in the occupation of buildings is unsustainable. There is a growing acceptance of the need for greater efficiency and environmental performance but current policies do not go far enough.

THE USE OF RESOURCES

Whilst buildings were built to last for centuries, now they are 'glued together' for a few decades, part of the throw-away society. Often the materials that are manufactured and used in these processes require much energy to produce them, they come from polluting and dangerous manufacturing processes and rely on plastics and synthetic chemicals. When they fall apart many of these materials end up in landfill sites as part of normal building practice, which is incredibly wasteful. Many buildings are regularly refitted with the previous interiors being stripped out and thrown away. Can the planet afford this method of building and what does it do to our health, our children and us?

Concern about these issues has led many to reconsider natural building because it seems to offer an antidote to the consumer society approach to building. It offers the prospect of returning to more timeless and traditional methods of building, added to which natural materials appear to be healthier, less polluting and available locally rather than being dependent on a global corporation and transport system. However, there are also many questions about this approach to building: can we build buildings to today's modern health and safety standards under the building regulations? Can we achieve the necessary levels of energy efficiency? Will the buildings be sound and stable? Will they keep out damp? Can we get anyone to give us a mortgage for natural buildings and will we be able insure them?

Misconceptions

There are those who assume that by using natural materials, lime, straw or earth, they will inevitably be able to build for much less than would normally be expected. Straw-bales are cheap so a straw-bale house must be cheap, it is assumed. There are also those who argue that natural buildings do not need to go through the normal planning and regulatory procedures. There are many misconceptions about the scientific principles behind natural building. Some talk about 'breathing walls' as though the air is whistling through them and others claim that mud walls provide high levels of insulation when they do not. This book tries to address some of these issues and raises some of the problems as well as the advantages of natural building. There is no point in being swept away by a blind enthusiasm for a building technique without being aware of its possible shortcomings. Being honest about the difficulties should not be seen as a negative thing, but as learning from mistakes and experience.

On the other hand, there are building surveyors, building societies and insurers who will jump on any problems with a 'told-you-so' mentality. These 'gatekeepers' to finance and approvals regard materials, which have been used for centuries, as high risk and are much happier to put their faith in unproven modern plastics and synthetic materials that will probably fall apart in ten years. They are easily swayed by the glossy, 'technical' literature of multinational companies with patents and accredited systems. Unfortunately it is hard to certify natural methods which rely on good practice on site and the careful selection of materials from the forest or the ground; this involves trust and care that are in short supply in today's construction industry.

It could be suggested that choosing natural building is to make a small protest against the globalization of everything and helping to behave in a responsible way about the environment. But it does not mean that we need to reject all the many highly useful and ingenious modern materials that have been developed and will help to make natural buildings work better. A sensible balance between old and new, manufactured and natural is probably the best basis for building so that we get the best of traditional and unprocessed materials and the best of clever technical innovation. A judgement about what to use should be based on sensible, pragmatic analysis and technical advice and the choice of the best things for the job in hand rather than an ideological perception that natural is right and manufactured is wrong.

If societies across the world could use such balanced judgement about when to choose low-impact solutions and restrict energy-consuming manufacturing processes to what was really essential, we would have fewer problems with pollution and global warming. Unfortunately, building a new cement or plastics factory is seen as progress, good for the economy and creating jobs. Developing countries in particular want to get away from buildings that symbolize a poverty of the past and instead aspire to the same standards that they see in the developed West. Instead we must try and develop low-impact solutions, not just because they are good for the environment, but also because they are best for building.

To quote Neil May, one of Britain's leading pioneers of natural building:

> New buildings and renovated buildings need to be built from low-energy, minimally processed bulk natural materials. Materials such as timber, earth, stone, straw and other natural fibres are not only the best materials from an environmental point of view, they are also the best materials from a performance point of view. Understood properly, they can and do provide houses which are simple to design, simple to build, simple to maintain, and which give health and satisfaction to those who live in them. This is not a step back to a pre-modern era. It is taking our modern understanding of material science and combining it with modern production techniques and modern designs, to make appropriate buildings for the twenty-first century.

National City Farms Headquarters Building in Bristol; architects: Architype, reflecting the important influence of Walter Segal on green building in Britain.

CHAPTER 2

Earth Building

In many ways earth is the most obvious material to use in natural building. Earth can be found everywhere and, as a result, it used to be said that the majority of the world's population still live in earth buildings. This may have changed in the last ten to twenty years as a result of rapid urbanization in Third World countries and the growth of cement manufacture. Of course, concrete and bricks are made of material from the earth, but what will be discussed here are buildings that are made out of earth in its most natural state with the minimum of treatment or processing.

Earth is not a renewable material and, once used in a building, cannot be renewed like timber, flax or hemp. On the other hand, when an earth building reaches the end of its life it can decay back to where it came from without doing any damage. This is particularly important in areas of the world where earth buildings may have a relatively short life as part of a nomadic existence and which, when abandoned, will not leave anything unpleasant behind. The extraction of earth, particularly on the site where the building is due to be constructed, is a zero-carbon solution to construction and earth walls and floors can be used as a direct substitute for mass concrete. The reduction of cement and concrete usage will have a direct and beneficial effect on reducing carbon emissions.

Sometimes suitable earth for building can be found on the site where the building is to be constructed. It may be necessary to excavate earth for the foundations, and this can be used for building if suitable. But suitable earth may not be available locally and thus must be transported some distance; this is also true of a range of earth-building products, which

bring with it a small burden of carbon emissions, although this will involve much less embodied energy than that used to make synthetic products. Where earth has to be transported it is necessary to ask the question whether another form of construction

Clay overburden from a quarry; much of this material goes to waste.

14

House and outbuildings with cob walling, by Kevin McCabe.

might be more environmentally responsible, as often it is possible to find other suitable earth nearby.

Earth building has a range of enthusiasts who are committed to just one form of construction and sometimes seem blind to other approaches. There are cob enthusiasts and rammed-earth enthusiasts, devotees of 'earthships' and of earth-sheltered buildings. The single-minded pursuit of cob or rammed earth has meant that there are now people with enormous expertise in these methods of construction, but, as with every other method discussed in this book, the reader is advised to keep an open mind and recognize that there is a wide range of materials and building systems to choose from and that often a combination of more than one approach is the best way to go. Earth plasters and finishes are now gaining in popularity and can be used in conjunction with earth walls or other materials.

Earth-sheltered buildings are not discussed here specifically as they use natural materials only incidentally and frequently rely on large amounts of concrete and synthetic waterproofing materials. Excellent pioneering earth-sheltered, green projects, such as the Hockerton Housing in Nottinghamshire which uses a big earth bank on the north side of a terrace of passive solar dwellings, have had a valuable educational influence. Earthships are buildings that use earth packed into disused tyres, sometimes in conjunction with earth sheltering. They can therefore claim to be recycling a material that presents a serious problem for disposal. However, there remain questions about this technology, which are discussed below.

Earth walls and floors have many possibilities for the natural builder. Getting closer to the natural earth is attractive to some and being surrounded by

A cob house in northern France being repaired and extended by using concrete blocks; it is not easy to get approval to knock down cob houses there, but the authorities seem unable to insist that the new work is in harmony with the old.

earth walls gives some a sense of well being that they do not get from manufactured materials. On the other hand there remain questions about durability, insulation and performance that mean that earth is not always the automatic choice.

COB BUILDING

History

Archaeologists can show us how early settlements in Britain used wattle and daub construction in which timber hurdles were plastered with mud mixed with vegetation such as straw, and animal dung. This provided a good protection from wind and rain. Over time more substantial and solid walled buildings were created with much thicker walls by using earth and straw mixed together. Mud-walled houses, as they are known in Ireland, were still being constructed in the

Cob house under construction in Somerset, up to first floor; builder: Kevin McCabe.

early part of the twentieth century. I have met men in County Tyrone who could describe the process and the tools from personal, hands-on experience when a whole community would get together to raise a house over a few days. Low-income farmers had to construct mud-houses since this was the only material to hand. The forests and the stone quarries belonged to the landlords and so roofs were restricted to short lengths of bog oak and foundations made from field-stones that could be gathered from nearby.

Sadly, poorly informed builders have destroyed many cob houses in Ireland. They have tried to inject silicone damp-proof courses into mud walls and plaster the outside with sand and cement renders. These interventions prevent the walls from breathing and make any damp problems worse. Many houses have been abandoned or demolished as a result of official replacement dwelling policies. But in the south-west and other parts of rural England the value of such buildings has been recognized and many have been lovingly restored. This book is not about the restoration of old buildings but it is important to note that the growth of cob restoration and the expertise it has developed has led to the realization that this might be a form of construction for the future. The fact that

well-maintained cob buildings have stood for hundreds of years has encouraged new cob builders that this is a sustainable form of construction, which can meet the aims of natural building. Where existing cob buildings are being restored or extended it would make sense to use natural materials and methods that are in sympathy with the existing materials.

Techniques of Cob Building

There are numerous books on cob building techniques produced in the United Kingdom and the USA, but, as with many natural building techniques, it is advisable for anyone wanting to design or build a cob building to go on a well-run, hands-on practical course. Getting your hands (and feet) dirty with cob, literally, is essential in order to understand how the material works. The basic technique is the same for any building in that earth and straw must be mixed together and the material then placed by hand to build up a wall of the appropriate thickness. The rough wall is then shaped to a relatively smooth finish by hand or with various tools. The final wall can be plastered or left unfinished internally and sometimes externally. True cob construction does not involve the use of shuttering or ramming and is

An historic cob cottage where dampness has been caused by inappropriate cement render. Only lime is suitable for earth walls.

Cob can be used in any sort of building, such as this rather elaborate bus shelter at the Eden project in Cornwall; by Jackie Abey and Jill Smallcombe. (Photo: Abey Smallcombe)

essentially a hand technique, although machinery can be used for mixing and lifting the cob into place. Cob lends itself to sculptural forms with relative ease and thus most cob buildings display a range of curves, and individual details reflect the taste of the builder. Cob builders feel that this technique is one of the most natural forms of construction because there is direct contact between the builder and the material without any mechanical intervention and the final result can be moulded with personality. While cob buildings can be designed and drawn, the temptation to change things on site is overwhelming and easy to do, so cob is the most 'plastic' method of building.

Cob building is mainly for walls, but it is possible to create floors by using a mix similar to that in the walls. Doors and window openings can easily be formed in cob walls. The walls themselves can be straight or battered and curved.

Materials

The earth used in cob is sub-soil and should contain little organic matter. When excavated on site, the topsoil should be removed and the sub-soil tested before use. Too much clay in the material is not good, but the soil mixture may be changed, by adding sand or some other material. If the mix is too rich in clay it will shrink and crack as the wall dries out; however, clay is necessary to give strength to the mix. A good sub-soil for cob would include 1 to 2 parts of clay to 1 part of silt or 'fines', 2 to 3 parts of sand and 3 to 4 parts of stone or gravel.

Soil can be tested on site in a variety of ways, either by hand or by using a jar test that will reveal its constituent parts. It is also important to test the material for shrinkage. Sand and gravel or clay can be added to get the right mix. Experienced cob builders can assess the materials that are available by eye and squeezing them in their hands, but for more scientific results it may be possible to get a university laboratory to carry out more tests.

Straw has to be added to the soil to act as a binder, giving greater strength and reducing shrinkage. The straw must be used straight from the bale and not chopped. The total mixture should include 2 to 3 per cent of straw. Wheat, barley or oat straw are used normally, but bracken or heather, hay or even fine twigs have been used in the past when no straw was available.

Ordinary clean water is added to the mixture and its amount can vary according to the sub-soil that is being used. It is important not to get the mix too wet since it will slump and fall off the wall. A proportion of 1 part of water to 4 parts of soil is normal, but this can vary quite a lot, hence the importance of getting good experience. It is vital to construct a test wall first before starting on the main building.

The mix is normally made on the ground, preferably near to where the walls are to be made. The cob mixture is heavy and normally involves quite a few people if it is to be done by hand. It is best to mix by hand on a large board with a manageable area to work. Some straw is laid down first, followed by the soil. The mix needs to be turned with a fork or a shovel and thoroughly mixed so that the straw is evenly distributed. Water, soil and straw are added in stages and the mix is then trodden with people 'jogging on the spot'. It is necessary to continue to turn the mix, which is hard but enjoyable work, especially in a group. It is not possible to use a cement mixer since the material is too sticky and it would be

Sometimes it is possible to use materials from the site of a building; in this project in Oxfordshire, the earth 'quarry' is in the foreground and the mixing area to the left of the building.

Kevin McCabe uses a digger to mix and lift the cob into place.

necessary to add far too much water. Traditionally, animals would have mixed cob so that dung would accidentally also have been added.

A less labour-intensive method is to use a mechanical wheeled digger. The material is spread with the digger's bucket and then the digger is driven backwards and forwards over the mixture. The bucket can scrape up the mix and turn it. It can then be lifted in the bucket and placed where required on the wall.

The Design of the Wall

Cob buildings must have good foundations and it is normal practice to have a plinth so that the cob wall starts about half a metre off the ground. If there is a good roof overhang this should ensure that splash from the roof hits only the plinth and not the cob wall. However, driving rain in Scotland and Ireland can soak a cob wall and a good lime render will also be required. Ideally, the plinth should be left exposed, but occasionally the render is taken right down to the ground. The foundations will need to be about 200mm wider than the wall and the plinth will need to be as wide as the cob. Most cob walls going up one or two storeys will be 450 to 500mm thick, but it is possible to create cob buildings with thinner walls if strength is not an issue. Cob walls have a great deal of mass but are not necessarily very strong.

Traditionally, the foundations and plinth would be made of rubble stone, often laid as a dry stone wall. There are advantages in the plinth and the foundations being able to drain naturally. Today the foundations will have to comply with modern regulations and are more likely to be made of concrete. The external finish of the plinth may be finished in natural stone but is sometimes built of concrete blocks. The foundation and the plinth can incorporate insulation (usually polystyrene) to help in meeting current building regulation requirements for energy efficiency. It is important to have a good French drain around the building to take away any water at the foot of the wall. Even though a conventional damp-proof course may be expected, cob builders would not regard this as good practice and the cob should bear on the plinth direct. If the footings and the plinth are constructed with limecrete and lime mortar (*see* Chapter 6) it is important to ensure that they have gained reasonable strength before the cob wall is begun.

Placing the Cob

The cob mixture is placed on the wall with forks or the bucket of the digger in lifts. These would normally be of 600mm in height for each lift. The cob is trodden into place to a rough shape and then

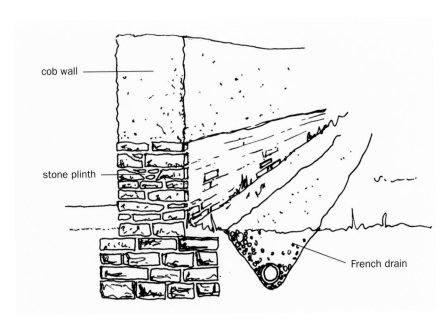

cob wall

stone plinth

French drain

A cob wall needs a good hat (the roof) and a good pair of boots, in this case a stone plinth with good drainage.

Rebecca Little, who is a cob building expert, can be seen here paring a new cob wall at Rowardennan, Loch Lomond in Scotland. (Photo: Rebecca Little)

Paring and thwacking or beating a wall to get a neat finish.

Kevin McCabe beating a cob chimney and stair wall.

whacked or kicked. The cob normally overhangs the plinth and is then pared back with a sharp spade or paring tool, but some overhang should remain. The cob material will shrink and this must be allowed for. A plumb line can be used if the wall is to be vertical. The wall is whacked with a paddle and the final finish can be adequate without any further work if it is done carefully. Further lifts are added, normally with a day or two between them. If the cob is to be exposed then the join at each lift will be apparent. The cob walls can be shaped and sculpted and niches and shelves built into it.

Wooden formwork is normally used to form window and door openings. This has to be strong and braced because the cob is heavy and will exert pressure on the timber. Some builders will build in timber grounds at the opening for fixing window and door frames. Lintels and beams can be built in and these can be of timber, concrete or steel.

Finishing Cob Walls

Cob walls may be plastered with clay or lime plasters both internally and externally. A good lime render will be essential where the wall is exposed to much

The cob wall at the Cobtun house in Worcester, built by Kevin McCabe, has been left naked and unrendered; the wall is largely north-facing and fairly sheltered.

driving rain, but in sheltered positions cob has been left unfinished. If the cob is damaged it is relatively easy to repair although the patch may be obvious. Stones and gravel in the mix will appear on the surface of the wall and will add to its texture and aesthetic quality. Some buildings have been constructed where the cob is left unplastered, partly for its aesthetic properties but also because it is believed that it will be sufficiently durable without a render. The award winning Cobtun house in Worcester, designed by Associated Architects, has a long cob wall which acts as a garden and partial house wall. It has been left unrendered and is largely on the sheltered north side of the building.

Opinions vary as to whether it is necessary to cover earth walls during construction when it rains. Covering can result in large areas of plastic sheeting flapping in the wind, which can even collect rain and spoil some of the construction. But it is important to ensure that each lift dries out before the next lift begins. Cob is not as vulnerable to rain as straw-bales, however.

Free-Standing Cob Walls

Cob has been used for free-standing boundary walls for many years. The coping on top of the wall is crucial for its survival since it needs to be much wider than a conventional coping in order to throw rain

Kevin McCabe has left the cob walls to his own house unrendered; however, he may decide to finish them with lime.

Becky Little's cob walls at the Rowardennan visitor centre have been finished with lime.

Michael Buck has covered his unfinished cob walls because heavy rain can cause damage to freshly laid material.

Cob bricks at Mike Wye Building Supplies in Devon, useful for repairing old cob walls but they can also be used in new build.

away from the wall. All cob walls require a good roof overhang so that water does not drip continually on to their bases or exposed corners.

Cob Bricks, Blocks, Balls and Sausages

It is possible to use the same mix as for normal cob walls and to form it into bricks or blocks. This can be done by hand or with a block-making machine. Such cob blocks are also available from some eco builders' merchants. They are mainly used for repairs to existing old cob buildings where a section of a wall has to be replaced. Earth or lime mortars are used between the blocks.

Cob buildings can be built by forming a cob mix into balls or various sausage shapes. These can be laid on top of each other to form a wall that can be easier to make than by lifting large weights of cob mixture. Some traditional buildings in Africa have used this method and surprisingly thin walls can be achieved in this way in domed buildings. Thinner walls can also be made by using the wattle and daub method where hazel or some other suitable timber hurdles are then plastered with a cob mixture that is pressed into place.

Thermal Insulation and Other Properties of Cob

'The common perception that earth is a very good material for thermal insulation cannot be proved'; this authoritative statement by Gernot Minke is part of an honest explanation of the thermal performance of earth. Essentially, the lighter the earth mixture and the more air trapped in it, the better the insulation. Heavy, dense, rammed earth walls have poor insulating properties, cob is somewhat lighter but only a little better. Lightweight straw/clay can give a U value (thermal transmittance) as good as $0.20W/m^2K$. However, cob and other earth walls have the beneficial properties of having a greater thermal capacity than lightweight insulations. They can store heat and also absorb moisture. These issues are discussed in a later chapter in which the 'decrement' or time-lag factor is explained. The experience of living in a cob building is that it will have a good level of thermal comfort and perform better than might be predicted from simply assessing the crude U value.

Cob walls are considered to be non-combustible, even with its straw content, by building standards in most countries such as Germany and the USA, but there are no technical guidelines for cob in the United Kingdom and so it may be necessary to cite standards from elsewhere.

From a structural point of view, cob walls are dependent on the composition of the earth and its binding strength. Cob has good compressive strength if built correctly, and there are earth buildings in the Yemen of ten storeys. The thickness and the mass of cob walls will be sufficient for two-storey buildings but specialist structural advice should be sought for unusual buildings of greater height or with thinner walls.

Earth-filled bags as a footing for a straw-bale wall, designed by Joe Kennedy at the Green Living Fair in Northern Ireland.

A light clay wall of straw and clay slip at Top Barn Training Farm near Worcester, built by Jim Wallis.

EARTH BAGS

Some experiments have been conducted in which bags are filled with earth or gravel and used both for foundations and walls. Placing the bags, if they are not too heavy, can be simpler for self-builders and some quite sophisticated structures have been achieved in this way, including domes. Bags are made of either natural materials or polypropylene. Polypropylene will degrade in sunlight, but natural, porous materials will make it possible to plaster the bag surfaces and to create a solid walled structure. Cob walls have been built on earth bag foundations and reinforcement between the cob and the bags has been formed with barbed wire or stakes driven into the bags. But reinforcement is particularly important in earthquake-prone areas.

LIGHT EARTH OR *LEICHTLEHM*

Looking somewhat similar to cob, light earth or straw clay construction consists of mixing straw, wood chips or other fibrous materials with a clay slip and placing it within shuttering. The clay slip is mixed in much the same way as cob but with more water. The light earth wall has a higher proportion of fibre such as straw incorporated than in cob and is thus not as heavy. It is a form of construction halfway between straw-bale and cob and rammed earth. It has a higher level of thermal insulation than cob and can protect the straw from fire and decay. Light clay blocks can also be made and are available commercially from eco builders' merchants. Some of these are manufactured in Germany and imported into Britain, which seems hard to justify when they can be so easily made on site. Light earth is not as strong as cob and can be used only as infill with timber structures. It is important to ensure that the mix dries out properly before it is plastered.

This form of construction was developed in Germany in the 1920s and has been popular since then. Wet 'loam', as it is known in Germany, with Gernot Minke as its leading expert, has the advantage that it can be extruded from machines or squeezed

27

The interior of Kevin McCabe's house demonstrates the sculptural possibilities of cob.

into nylon stockings to create different profiles. The material can be pumped and has even been mixed with expanded clay to give greater insulation. The possibilities seem endless.

Cob and Earth Interiors

Because of its plastic nature, cob and other earth building methods can open a wide range of possibilities for the interior of buildings. Interior finishes can range from simply leaving the cob or light clay walls exposed, to earth and lime plasters. Shapes can be moulded into the walls and shelves and niches can be built in.

Staircases and Earth Floors

Solid staircases and ground floors can be constructed with the same material as cob walls. Underfloor heating is incorporated in some cob floors and floors and staircases can be tiled. In the following sequence of pictures (*see* pp. 30 and 31), very rough cob stairs can be seen at an early stage, when almost completed and then with the final tiling.

UNFIRED EARTH BRICKS

The discovery that clay, mixed with straw or wood binders, can be extruded has led to the development of unfired earth bricks. Unfired, hand-made and machine-pressed bricks are now available commercially, imported from Germany or made in Britain. Lightweight bricks can have a reasonable insulation value but may not be suitable for external use.

OPPOSITE: Shelves and other light elements can be built into cob walls during construction.

Underfloor or wall heating can be incorporated into cob walls and floors without difficulty.

BELOW AND OPPOSITE: These images show how what begins as very rough-and-ready cob stairs can become an elegant, tiled staircase in the hands of Kevin McCabe.

Light clay straw bricks on display at Construction Resources in London.

Extruding unfired earth bricks at the Errol Brick Co. in Perthshire; the bricks are dried with waste heat.

Machine-made, unfired earth bricks are usually heavier and denser than hand-made bricks, and are being made by at least one British brick company. The same clay is used as for normal bricks but is mixed with either some straw or wood fibre and then extruded from a machine to form ordinary looking bricks; the only difference is that they are not fired in a kiln.

The bricks must either be dried in air or with waste heat from a normal brick kiln.

Adobe bricks are manufactured in large quantities in the USA today. These are unburnt bricks dried in the sun, adopted in the USA from Mexico, but ultimately Arabic. Adobe is used throughout the world either in hand- or machine-made form and is probably the most commonly used material for building construction. However, fired bricks are much more common in Britain and are associated with the best quality form of building, but despite attempts to recover heat and make much more energy-efficient kilns, brick making is a significant source of carbon dioxide emissions.

There are not many examples of buildings made with unfired bricks in the United Kingdom, but an important piece of research has been carried out by Tom Morton of Arc Architects in Scotland, which investigated the potential for this product. In the project, the unfired earth bricks have been used as infill to a timber-frame wall to give thermal mass and the substrate for the internal finishing plaster. Timber-frame structures, even if well insulated with lightweight insulation quilts, suffer from a lack of thermal mass since there is little to hold any heat except perhaps the floor if it is solid.

The Arc Architects' study is one of the few recent in-depth pieces of research into the performance of this innovative form of construction and considers the ability of the unfired earth to regulate moisture, thermal performance, acoustic, structural, buildability, and so on. The unfired bricks provide little insulation and so pumped cellulose insulation was used. The walls were treated internally with a clay plaster and the timber frame was clad externally with timber boarding. The building was carefully monitored once it had been constructed and much data is available in a report (*see* References: Morton *et al.*). The study found that the unfired bricks had only 14 per cent

Unfired earth bricks used for internal walls of a house at Dalguise, Perthshire; designed by Arc Architects. (Photo: Tom Morton)

Earth plaster applied to the unfired earth bricks at Dalguise. (Photo: Tom Morton)

of the embodied energy of fired bricks; the bricks themselves are inexpensive and should be useful in low-cost construction; the moisture-control perform-ance was good, particularly in the bathroom where the brick walls were able to absorb moisture; and the energy performance was 30 per cent better than that predicted by the U value calculations. Unfired earth bricks have been used only as infill in the Scottish project where they performed no structural role,

though they would have provided bracing between the timber studs. However, unfired earth bricks do have structural properties and might be used in load-bearing construction in the future.

RAMMED EARTH

This is another form of unfired earth construction in which walls and building elements are created

Rammed chalk wall at the Kindersley Centre, Sheepdrove Organic Farm, Lambourn, Berkshire; architects: Alec French Partnership.

without using heat. Moist sub-soil is compacted into formwork in layers and then rammed for compaction. Rammed earth has been used in many parts of the world for centuries, including in the Great Wall of China, where compaction was done by hand, but today pneumatic mechanical ramming devices are available. Once the earth has been compacted, the shuttering is removed and the walls allowed to dry naturally.

Rammed earth is popular for its aesthetic properties since a wide range of colours and textures can be obtained. Because rammed earth is compacted into layers, the layers themselves become visible once the shuttering has been removed, providing attractive patterns and textures. The colour and appearance of the earth depends on the local soil, sands and gravel in the mixture, so in some parts of the south of England rammed earth walls can be rammed chalk walls.

As with other earth walls, rammed earth provides good thermal mass and has the hygroscopic properties that enable it to absorb moisture. Rammed earth is stiffer and stronger than cob or adobe and can carry considerable structural loads. Walls are very durable if properly protected from driving rain and can appear almost to have turned to stone. The

rammed earth walls at the visitor centre at the Centre for Alternative Technology were covered with transparent sheets to prevent inquisitive visitors from picking off bits of earth, but now the wall is so solid that this is no longer a problem. The rammed earth wall absorbs significant amounts of solar gain from south-facing roof lights and helps to keep the building warm. The top of the wall has a lime-stabilized section to give added strength, since the weight of the timber roof bears on the wall.

Unlike cob construction, rammed earth needs a greater amount of technical expertise in terms of designing and constructing shuttering and should not be attempted by self-builders without proper instruction and engineering advice. The force of ramming can easily push off the shuttering if it is not properly braced and fixed. Erecting the shuttering and constructing lifts, which must be allowed to dry before proceeding with the next section, means that rammed earth building is not much faster than cob; but rammed earth walls can support significant structures and can even be formed into columns.

Such walls need normally to be at least 200mm thick and care must be taken to check the slenderness ratio for high walls, requiring greater thickness as the

35

Rammed earth wall at the Centre for Alternative Technology in Wales; the lime-stabilized top layer is for the timber roof structure to bear on.

Earth is packed into shuttering and then rammed with a vibrating ram.

walls go higher. Walls can be shaped into curves and circles but this is limited by the shuttering. The strength of the walls will also be affected by the quality of the sub-soil and in some parts of the world cement is added to stabilize the mix. Adding cement, of course, reduces the environmental benefits of an otherwise low embodied-energy and pollution-free building solution. Normally, rammed earth walls are constructed in situ but it is possible to create prefabricated rammed earth elements. In Austria one can order fireplace walls and other elements, such as a church altar, that are factory-made and delivered to site.

Shuttering or formwork can be made up on site with strong marine plywood and braced with timber posts. Normally, the shuttering is connected through the walls with rods that are bolted on each side. Specialized shuttering has been developed in some countries where rammed earth is commonly used. Care has to be taken when removing the shuttering as it can damage the finish of the walls.

Rammed earth is not cheap because of the need for shuttering and the labour involved, but it can be comparable with conventional masonry. There can be problems with the durability of rammed earth where damage is caused through impact or rainwater, and erosion can occur and, for this reason, rammed earth is often used in situations where there is a glazed or some other form of rain screen to protect the wall. Erosion can also result from poor sub-soil or poor detailing, but, as with most forms of construction, good design and care can obviate most problems. As with cob, rammed earth does not provide a good level of thermal insulation and it is necessary to add insulation to external walls to achieve a good standard. Rammed earth walls, however, can provide excellent heat stores in passive solar design.

The soils used in rammed earth can vary in terms of local availability, either from the construction site or from nearby quarries. Straw or other fibres are not normally added, as with cob, but the colour and

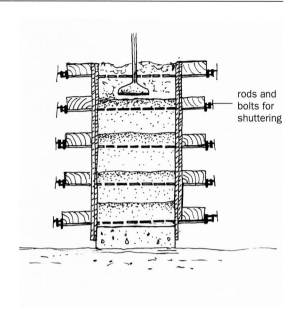

rods and bolts for shuttering

Section showing how rammed earth is built up in layers; the rods bolting the shuttering together will leave holes when they are removed.

RIGHT: A prefabricated section of rammed earth wall, built by Martin Rauch in Austria but on display at Construction Resources in London.

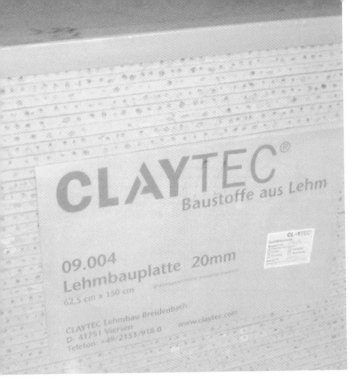

appearance can vary with the addition of gravel, stone and coloured sands.

The principles of detailing rammed earth is similar to cob construction. A good overhanging roof is required to keep driving rain off the wall but defects can occur due to erosion if weathering is severe. All of these issues are fully explained with technical guidance on structural and construction methods in a guide produced by Pete Walker and others and published by the Building Research Establishment.

EARTH PLASTERS AND FINISHES

A wide range of earth plasters are now commercially available and are discussed further in Chapter 9. Many contain coloured additives and may be quite expensive, but they do provide an excellent alternative to normal plasters and paint. It is also possible to make earth plasters and renders by using earth mixes as in cob construction. The addition of straw or other fibres can improve the strength of the mixture, but

Claytec earth and reed boards at the Natural Building Technologies warehouse; Claytec also make earth plasters.

Second-hand tyres rammed with chalk earth at the Earthship project in Brighton.

not too much should be added to maintain workability. Clay plasters have been used externally in the United Kingdom and Ireland but their durability is not yet proven. Clay building boards are now available as an alternative to plasterboard and can be used as a substrate to clay plasters.

EARTH-FILLED TYRES

A number of natural builders have found earth-filled tyres useful for footings or for retaining walls. It sounds like a useful way of making use of a toxic waste product that has now become a major disposal problem. Unfortunately, their use in buildings is unlikely to make a dent in the tyre mountain. Ramming earth into tyres is also an unpleasant, time-consuming and difficult job and not everyone will feel that the final result is particularly attractive. However, the tyres are strong and can be stacked, when filled with earth, to create walls and are particularly useful as retaining or external walls.

Earth and tyre walls are sometimes used in houses and buildings that are occupied by people. There is little conclusive evidence as to the level of emissions of the many toxic chemicals used in tyres so this may be an acceptable practice. Plastering with earth may not reduce any emissions, if they do exist, as the earth is a breathing material. Anyone considering this form of construction will have to decide for themselves whether this is an appropriate contribution to natural building.

HOLLOW FIRED EARTH BRICKS

Hollow or perforated fire earth bricks or blocks are commonly used throughout Europe, particularly to infill walls in concrete frame structures. Often known as 'Poraton' blocks, these were manufactured in the

Fired hollow clay blocks in a demonstration breathing-wall eco-house at Natural Building Technologies.

United Kingdom and Ireland until they were dropped for having insufficient compressive strength. As with fired bricks, these materials require some energy for their manufacture, but are nevertheless being promoted as a useful ecological and natural building material. The blocks provide some thermal insulation and are light and easy to build with, by using a thin mortar joint. They can be combined with other low-impact materials for ecological building and are being offered by one or two companies as an economical solution to low-energy solid wall construction.

CHAPTER 3

Timber Building

TIMBER: THE MOST NATURAL MATERIAL

Timber is perhaps the oldest natural material used in building after cave dwellings. A simple shelter can be made from sticks, branches and leaves. It is hard to conceive of a modern building that would not include timber in some form. It is not only an adaptable and flexible material which can be used for a range of purposes from structure to internal and external finishes, doors, windows, fixtures and fittings, but it is also a material which imparts a strong natural feeling to any building, softening its impact. The aesthetic appeal of timber is interpreted in many ways and even 'brutalist' concrete buildings are sometimes designed so that the timber patterns of shuttering appear on the concrete.

Timber is also a renewable material and is regarded as good for the environment as the world's forests are an essential part of the planetary ecosystem, absorbing carbon dioxide and emitting oxygen. It would therefore seem inevitable that natural buildings should use timber to be both beautiful and environmentally responsible. However, timber is a valuable resource that should be used responsibly and the natural builder should try to use it efficiently. When timber is used it should be in a way that expresses its beauty and character and where it is the best material for the job. It remains one of the most natural and beautiful of materials and will always be at the heart of any natural building project.

OPPOSITE: Houses made from recycled timber whiskey vats at the Findhorn Community in Scotland.

WAYS OF USING TIMBER

Timber can be used in a number of ways in natural buildings and to do justice to this subject would require another book, but, for present purposes, a few examples are discussed, which represent some of the main uses of timber associated with natural and ecological building; these are:

- timber framing
- round wood, green timber and grid shells
- timber cladding
- composite and innovative timber products.

TIMBER SOURCING

It is wrong to assume that all timber is acceptable from an environmental point of view. The natural builder should show a great deal of care, responsibility and respect when using it. It is wrong to assume that, since all timber is renewable, wood may be used in a free and uncontrolled way. In recent years the timber trade has campaigned to promote the use of timber as sustainable and environmentally friendly and preferable to other materials. The 'Wood for Good' and other marketing campaigns have done this very successfully. However, the statement trotted out by the timber suppliers that all their wood is from sustainable sources should be regarded with the same scepticism as 'the cheque is in the post'.

It is often argued that any wood used can be replaced through the planting of more trees, ignoring the reality that trees take fifty to eighty years to grow and become useful again for construction purposes. At an international level forests are now being cut

41

The Kindersley Centre is a conference and educational centre promoting organic farming and food, but also demonstrates innovative natural building using timber as well as rammed chalk.

down to meet the voracious demands of growing economies, not just for construction but for fuel, paper and many other purposes. Frequently timber is used for pulping and purposes, for which it is not very efficient and creates chemical waste, when other forms of cellulose such as hemp would be much better. Crops, such as hemp, can produce cellulose on an annual basis without damaging the soil, whereas a forest once felled can create terrible environmental problems, leading to an increase in mudslides and flooding. There is also a thriving black market in illegally logged timber, much of which finds its way to the United Kingdom.

Thus an environmentally responsible approach to timber is to use it thoughtfully and in moderation when it is providing real benefit to a building. The timber industry promotes the idea that the use of more timber will significantly reduce carbon emis-

sions. This is not such a straightforward argument as it might appear because it depends on what the timber is replacing, whether forests are being replanted at a much greater rate than is currently the case and the fossil fuel energy being used shipping timber and timber products around the world. On the other hand, there are some important projects in poorer tropical countries where the local people are benefiting from the sustainable management and harvesting of timber and these initiatives should be supported.

As a general rule, however, if the timber can be sourced locally from a forest where it needs to be cleared anyway, as part of its thinning and management, this is a much more attractive proposition to the natural builder than the use of wood that has arrived on a truck from the other side of the world. There are also many forms of quick growing timber such as bamboo and indigenous British woods, such

A Woodmizer mobile sawmill can be towed to woodland or a site and used to cut local timber used either green or left to season.

as hazel and willow, that can be used in buildings after just a few years of growth. Thus the natural builder should be looking to use timber economically and responsibly by taking the time and trouble to select and source it carefully.

The use of recycled timber is another way to reduce the wasteful consumption of wood, and far too often timber is thrown away or burned when old buildings are demolished. Often old timber will be of better quality than new and, when used sensibly, can enhance the appearance of a natural building.

There are also a growing number of innovative, composite timber products that can be very useful in buildings but are not always as natural as they may appear to be. Some products are made from sawdust and wood waste and exploit natural resins and the lignin in timber instead of synthetic and toxic glues. Some innovative composites have the benefit of reducing the amount of timber that is used in them. For instance, a composite I-beam made from small strips of softwood and a flange of composite board made from chips of wood glued together, plywood or hardboard, can span quite large distances, whilst a solid piece of timber achieving the same span would use far more timber.

TIMBER CERTIFICATION

If timber or timber products are being bought from a merchant, the best way to be sure that the material

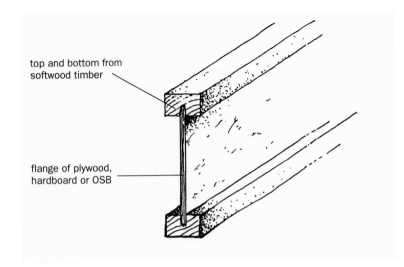

A timber I-beam with the top and bottom made from small-section softwood and the flange from plywood, hardboard or oriented strand board (OSB); it is possible to span large spaces with these lightweight beams and the greater depth allows more space for insulation and services.

top and bottom from
softwood timber

flange of plywood,
hardboard or OSB

has come from a properly managed and responsible source is if it has been certified by the Forest Stewardship Council (FSC). FSC certification is an expensive and complex process that involves visiting and independently checking on the management of forests and also certifying the producers and the supply chain. Because of the effort and costs involved, many in the trade avoid certification or subscribe to less convincing certification schemes. If you have any queries about this you can approach the FSC, but currently this is the only credible standard available. Many state forests are FSC-certified and you can obtain certified timber from many builders and timber merchants. If you are cutting your own wood from a local forest this may not be certified and you will have to ensure yourself that the woodland is being maintained sustainably. One of the main attractions of the FSC is that it is a global system, with a head office in Mexico and regional offices throughout the world. As the timber trade becomes increasingly global it is becoming much more difficult to check on certification systems in the USA, Canada or South-East Asia, but FSC can help with this.

TIMBER INSTEAD OF OTHER MATERIALS?

Many people are prejudiced against timber because they believe that it will rot, be attacked by insects or

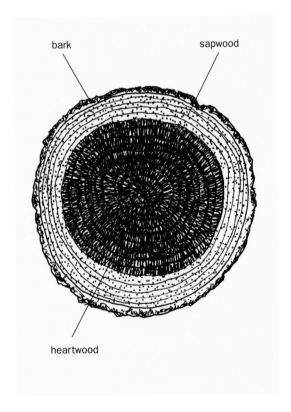

bark

sapwood

heartwood

Typical cross-section of a timber log; the central heartwood is the best for good quality timber but the newer sapwood may be used in composite products.

be more vulnerable in a fire. This prejudice was encouraged by a 'World in Action' television documentary on suspect timber-frame building practices in the 1960s. There was a tendency in the construction industry to treat timber in the same way as synthetic materials, and even today it is possible to see timber incorrectly used where it cannot breathe or dry out when wet.

Timber has been heavily treated with toxic chemicals in the past in the belief that this would protect it from rot and insect attack. Many building societies and banks still enforce the spraying of timber each time a house changes hands because of a dependence on the value of timber-treatment guarantees. But like most natural materials, timber will last a long time if it is used properly and is of good quality. Timber which is largely made of sapwood is more prone to decay and insect attack. Timber can get wet and still recover if it is able to dry out again, and even where there are terrible problems such as dry rot, this can now be treated without the use of toxic chemicals, if the dry rot fungus is starved of food, and old wood can be saved or reused.

Many people have taken out their old timber windows, even when they could have been repaired, and replaced them with uPVC windows. These are advertised as maintenance-free and even better for the environment, but there is now plenty of evidence that uPVC is one of the most damaging materials currently in widespread use. The arguments are well summarized in a report produced by the World Wide Fund for Nature (WWF) and anyone considering uPVC should read it. There are now suppliers of high-performance, energy-efficient windows that are also FSC-certified. While they are more expensive than other windows, they will help to make a building look good and also be more energy efficient.

Natural builders are unlikely to use uPVC because it looks terrible, but this does not mean that we should be completely biased against plastics. There are a growing number of alternative plastic products, some made from synthetic materials that are not as damaging as PVC, and others from recycled plastics. I have used recycled plastic 'planks' for raised beds in my garden because it is made from supermarket packaging and even when being in constant contact with wet soil will not rot. The use of 'plastic lumber', as it is called in the USA, can be a way to reduce the use of timber except where it is the most appropriate choice.

POST AND BEAM TIMBER FRAME

There are many forms of timber-frame construction for buildings. Timber-frame buildings can be built to

Plastic lumber used for a raised bed in a vegetable garden; in some circumstances recycled plastic can be used as an alternative and save trees.

A high-quality, high-performance timber window painted, stained or oiled with natural finishes is preferred in natural buildings to metal or uPVC; this window is at the Wintles eco-housing development in Shropshire.

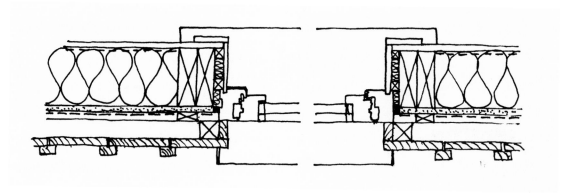

A plan of typical window detail in a timber frame.

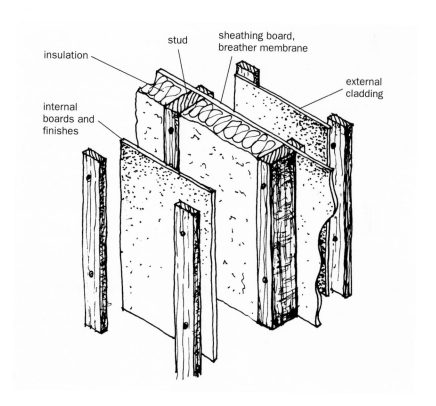

insulation

stud

sheathing board,
breather membrane

external
cladding

internal
boards and
finishes

*This drawing shows
the complexity of
conventional timber-
frame build up.*

five or six storeys, but such structures consume a great deal of wood. An increasing number of companies offer a range of timber-frame packages, and timber panels can be prefabricated and delivered to site so that a house or small building can be erected in a day or two. Trussed rafters and other prefabricated roof sections have been used for many years. The UK Timber Frame Association has reported a big increase in the use of timber-frame construction (up 18 per cent in 2004), with a market share of 17 to 20 per cent in England and over 60 per cent in Scotland.

47

Timber building at CAT in Wales, where Segal frame building courses are run.

Natural builders, on the other hand, have avoided standard solutions because it is not always possible to be sure of the quality of timber used in package deal timber-frame kits and few of them currently offer FSC-certified timber. It is also necessary to use a lot of timber in panelized and stud framing, far more than is structurally efficient, if greater wall thicknesses are required for higher levels of insulation.

On the other hand, a prefabricated section of wall panels arriving on site may save much time and be economical. Some timber-frame companies will work with natural builders and not object to suggestions of cutting out toxic chemicals and the use of innovative and natural insulation solutions. It is best to work out the design and then shop around to find a timber-frame supplier who is flexible and also environmentally responsible.

More companies are now offering timber package houses that consist of structurally insulated panels (SIPS). SIPS consist of a wood chip, wafer or other composite board, which is bonded to a synthetic insulation material such as polystyrene or polyisocyanurate. Some ecological architects and builders have experimented with this form of construction, since it is possible to achieve very energy-efficient and airtight forms of construction which can be prefabricated and quickly erected on site. Unfortunately, natural insulation products cannot be used in this

The form of post and beam construction pioneered by Walter Segal has been influential in the natural building movement; the posts sit on simple foundations with minimal ground disturbance and the frame gives great flexibility.

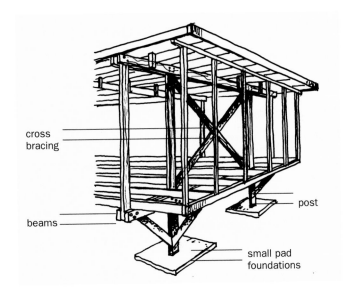

cross bracing

beams

post

small pad foundations

48

The Hedgehog self-build co-operative built this timber-frame house in Brighton in a small development inspired by Walter Segal.

way and thus SIPS do not really meet the criteria for natural building. Synthetic foam-type insulations are made from fossil fuels with environmentally-damaging fire retardants, adhesives and foaming agents. It is possible to use natural renewable products, such as rape oil and castor oil, as the polyol base, and natural alternatives to the cyanide chemicals have been produced in the laboratory, but the latter are not commercially available, as more scientific research is required. Foam insulation can be produced from natural starch, but this is also at a very early stage of development.

An alternative favoured by many green builders has been the post and beam construction made popular by Walter Segal and the Segal Self Build Trust. It is a more economical use of timber and allows for much greater flexibility. While the main posts and beams are of large sections, wall infills, windows and

doors can be placed more freely and internal walls can be taken down and moved if necessary. Panels between the posts can then be constructed by using conventional studwork for both internal and external walls. The great advantage of post and beam construction is that the roof can be put in place at an early stage of the construction process and any natural or vulnerable materials can then be protected from rain over the following weeks or months.

The Walter Segal method involves using a modular grid for the design of a house based on the standard 2,400mm by 1,200mm sizes of cladding panels and plasterboard. If used correctly, the amount of cutting and wastage can be reduced. A variety of insulation materials can be used with timber studwork and post and beam and these are normally encapsulated behind sheathing boards made from natural fibres (*see* below). Breather membranes are normally used,

49

which provide weather protection as well as allowing vapour permeability. Many of these membranes are made from synthetic plastic materials but more environmentally-friendly alternatives are available, such as bitumen-impregnated and other wood fibreboards. External cladding can range from bricks and blocks to timber boarding. Hemp insulation can also be cast around the timber frame, providing a solid wall form of construction. Each of these options is discussed below.

Even the disciples of Walter Segal have not followed his method slavishly and there are many projects where the Segal influence can be detected but where it has been adapted, particularly to create higher standards of insulation. Post and beam construction has proved to be popular with self-builders who can erect the frame with help from others and then complete the roof and work on the rest of the

building in the dry. The early Segal dwellings were not particularly well insulated, but more recent post and beam constructions have moved towards thicker walls. Double stud construction using very small sections of timber can be used in conjunction with post and beam for a more efficient use of timber for thicker, well insulated walls; developed by Andy Warren in Wales, double stud represents an efficient use of timber.

TRADITIONAL OAK AND LARGE SECTION FRAMING

Post and beam construction is normally formed with conventional, standard-sized, softwood, rectangular timber sections. This timber is normally vacuum dried (which uses much energy) and frequently treated with chemicals. The standard sections are

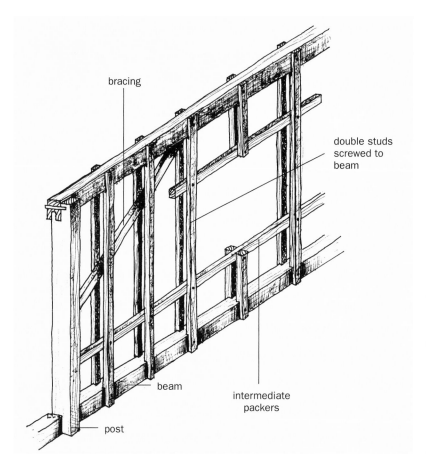

bracing

double studs screwed to beam

beam

intermediate packers

post

Double-stud construction makes it possible to use small sections of timber in conjunction with a post and beam frame to create thicker walls, with more insulation, while minimizing the use of timber. (Drawing based on the work of Andy Warren)

50

An oak-frame building under construction, showing concrete blocks in the background; not all traditional frame buildings are necessarily natural or ecological.

stress graded and it is easy for the structural engineer and local building control to give approval.

However, the use of alternative timber construction techniques is becoming more popular in which large sections of locally-sourced hardwood are used to create the main frame of a building. In many cases this is done to create something similar to the traditional, 'half-timbered' houses that were common in the Middle Ages. But architects and engineers have also designed sophisticated frames that use modern, high technology bolting and jointing techniques to create some very exciting buildings.

Oak-frame buildings have become fashionable in recent years and some systems are very expensive.

Many are used in buildings that otherwise exhibit few ecological or other natural features. Frames are also made from other indigenous woods such as Douglas fir, larch and sweet chestnut.

Traditional timber-frame construction of this kind is usually created with mortise and tenon joints and timber dowels. Often the timber can move and split, but this is generally accepted as part of the character of this technique and has to be allowed for in the design of the other building elements. Because the timber is rarely stress-graded and also for the desired appearance, traditional frame buildings can use a great deal more wood than is structurally necessary. If the timber is imported then this raises questions of

A small oak-frame building by Border Oak, a company operating since 1980 in Herefordshire, both working with architects and selling off-the-peg house types, some of which are designed to be affordable within a low budget. (Photo: Border Oak Ltd)

environmental responsibility, but many of the specialist companies in England and Wales now source their timber from FSC-certified local supplies.

Traditional oak and hardwood frame buildings may have problems in meeting higher insulation and energy-efficiency standards if structural elements go right through the wall and can act as a cold bridge. As the timber dries out and shrinks, great care must be taken to ensure that the walls stay air-tight. However, it does not make sense to spend much money on such a framing method only to cover it up with other materials. Companies, such as Border Oak in Herefordshire, offer a design and build service using oak frames with a range of approaches in which the visibility of the frame can vary. A key to these buildings

is the use of a weather-stripping detail claimed to allow the frame to move while retaining a watertight seal, which is a long way from the traditional vernacular detail. A solid wall, single insulated skin is also used. The Arts and Crafts style of many oak frame standard designs may not appeal to all tastes, but the techniques can be used in a more modern way if required.

An interesting hybrid of the traditional frame appearance with modern structural design and highly energy-efficient standards can be found at The Wintles, in Shropshire. This speculative development exhibits many interesting features, including car-free zones around the houses, communal allotment areas and other ecological features. Bob Tomlinson, the

A view of the Wintles, where houses are gathered around a communal, car-free, green area; the houses have a feeling of traditional oak frame combined with modern prefabricated timber framing.

developer, was keen to make the buildings as ecological as possible, but they have also made some compromises to meet the requirements of the National House Building Council (NHBC) warranty scheme. The houses, which are oriented to get the benefit of passive solar design, are three- and four-storey timber frame in which some aspects of the timber frame are expressed externally. The buildings also have lime render and timber cladding, with a relatively high standard of insulation. Recycled materials have been used to some extent as well as natural and low-toxicity paints and finishes. Heat recovery and active solar installations are also used to try and ensure a good standard of energy efficiency beyond that required by current regulations.

Much of the construction involves prefabrication in a large shed on site and a high specification is followed throughout in terms of air-tightness, high-performance windows and low-impact interior finishes. The Wintles is an interesting case of a project that exhibits natural materials but would also appeal to potential purchasers at the higher end of the market.

MODERN STRUCTURAL FRAMES

Some natural buildings use a form of construction in which traditional cruck frame and other forms create exciting frames expressed on the inside of buildings;

Conference hall at the Kindersley Centre with large span created by a modern cruck frame; architects Alec French Partnership and Mark Lovell Design Engineers.

this allows for more poetic and beautiful forms, adding to their character. These can also use traditional jointing and pegging methods or involve more high-tech steel fixings and connectors. While many structural engineers are firmly rooted in the use of steel and concrete, there are now architects and engineers who are willing to use timber in more exciting and innovative ways.

In modern buildings the timber frame is usually expressed in the interior and, with careful design, exciting large-span spaces can be created with frames made from local hardwood or even softwood. With the use of modern steel connectors and bolts, the

efficiency of the timber is greatly enhanced. While this does not have the simple elegance or romanticism of traditional pegs and dowels, the timber is used much more efficiently while retaining a traditional timber-frame appearance.

The Kindersley Centre in Berkshire is a conference centre that promotes organic farming and other environmental activities. The building was intended to demonstrate a similarly responsible approach to building, and while not all elements can be described as following natural building principles, the total impact is very effective, combining an adventurous timber frame internally, low-impact insulation, timber

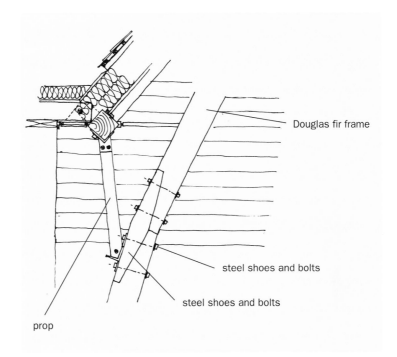

Detail of the steel shoes and props used in the Kindersley frame; architects Alec French Partnership and Mark Lovell Design Engineers.

Douglas fir frame

steel shoes and bolts

steel shoes and bolts

prop

cladding, a shingle roof and rammed chalk walls, and so it appears here in several chapters. The structure of the main spaces at the Kindersley Centre has been created with a parabolic arch, which mimics a traditional cruck frame. The frame is made up of 4.5m lengths of solid Douglas fir from a locally grown source. Jointing splices were formed with laminated Douglas fir and the purlins are also made from Douglas fir. Specially fabricated steel shoes are used to accommodate props and threaded rods were employed to adjust the position on site. The external cladding is of western red cedar and the insulation is of mineral wool. The shingles on the roof came from Canada and so it was not possible to build the whole building from local materials.

This simple and robust detailing of the timber at the Kindersley Centre is modern and yet respects the natural character of the timber.

This modern cruck frame in a house in mid Wales creates an interesting form; since it is at 90 degrees to the gable of the building, the fixings are more discreet; designer: Andy Warren.

Large section timber frames can also be used in domestic construction and impart a special character to even small buildings. Such a frame can create the main structure not just for the roof but the whole building, as has been achieved in a house in mid Wales designed by Andy Warren. The frame is seen most clearly at first-floor level, but it also goes through to the ground floor.

As with the Kindersley Centre, Douglas fir has been used, but here the jointing is much more discreet. The cruck frame creates an exciting two-storey space. The general feel of the building is dominated by timber both inside and out and, since the designer is based in the same building as the British FSC

headquarters, he could hardly avoid using certified timber throughout.

ROUNDWOOD AND GRIDSHELL

The building trade normally expects conventional sawn timber to be stress-graded, kiln-dried and impregnated with preservatives. Indeed, as much as possible seems to be done to remove the natural qualities of wood. Some American companies are now heat-treating timber to such an extent that it is claimed that preservatives are no longer needed. However, for the natural builder it is the natural

The cruck frame of the house in mid Wales is not evident externally, but, while there has been no attempt to disguise the modern against the old cottage, the new extension does not look out of place.

qualities of timber that makes it so attractive, with all its quirks and problems; its smell, its flaws and variations are part of the delight.

One of the most natural ways to use timber is not in a rectangular sawn form but in its natural, round-wood state. By sawing logs into rectangular pieces we take away much of the fibrous strength of timber and therefore waste wood with off-cuts, sawdust and lose its natural strength. Round-wood poles make it possible to use relatively 'poor' quality, local timber and create a natural appearance for the building. The classic form of this is the traditional log cabin used by pioneers in Canada and the United States before sawmills were established. Log cabins could be built with an axe and gaps and holes filled up with earth, much like ancient wattle and daub buildings. Log cabins are making a comeback in the United Kingdom and Ireland and are widely available from package-deal timber suppliers, although most of these are importing systems from the Baltic. However, they are not recommended here as a useful form of natural building since in almost every instance they represent a form of construction that is not using the timber for its natural qualities. To use logs for walls is a terrible waste of wood and the logs themselves can be subject to a serious weathering problem because the end grain is left exposed and rain gets into the horizontal joints (*see* page 58). In some cases local planning authorities are even requiring the logs to be covered in wire mesh and rendered with cement.

Round-wood timber is best used structurally for the main frame, walls and roof of buildings. This is one of the most efficient ways of using wood since the natural strength of the timber in the round is employed. One of the most elegant examples of this

Log cabin construction is designed to create the impression of the Wild West, but detailing does not always stand up to our weather.

can be seen in Ben Law's Woodland House in Sussex. The Woodland House is well explained in the book of the same name, which is strongly recommended to anyone interested in natural building since it explains and demonstrates a wide range of building techniques, including straw-bale walling, shingle roofing and earth plasters. Law shows how a house can be built from materials which are on your doorstep (in a rural context) and how green round wood timber in its natural form can be selected and thinned from woodland as part of its normal management. Each piece of sweet chestnut was selected by him to do a particular job, with natural twists and bends in the poles used to perform a particular job in the frame (*see* page 60).

Ben Law's Woodland House in Sussex uses a round-wood pole cruck frame; many of the other timber elements are from sweet chestnut poles, cut from the surrounding forest. (Photo: Stephen F. Morley)

Ben Law's house when finished, with timber boarding on the outside; some of the poles are still visible. (Photo: Stephen F. Morley)

The Woodland House uses sweet chestnut poles to create cruck frames as the main structure to form a kind of A-frame house with a lean-to along one side. The cruck frames were winched into place, not without some difficulty, by hand. Little energy was wasted on cutting and sawing and the whole structure is very economical as well as beautiful. The house uses natural insulation and finishes and timber for cladding and roofing.

The use of green timber, straight from the forest, will create some problems with movement and possible cracks appearing as the timber dries out, but this merely contributes to the character of the building. Choosing natural building means accepting the need for regular attention and adjustment to buildings, not assuming that it will require no maintenance for decades.

Experiments with round-wood construction have been carried out at Hooke Park in Dorset for a number of years and several innovative buildings were created there before the college closed. It is now being run by the Architectural Association School of Architecture. Hooke Park showed that relatively poor quality timber in the round could be used for quite sophisticated structures, and this has been explored further by the engineers and designers Buro Happold (*see* page 60).

GRID-SHELL CONSTRUCTION

Following work on round-wood poles at Hooke Park, another highly efficient form of timber construction of interest to natural builders was developed by Buro Happold, using small dimension timber in the form

Even for a relatively small house, putting up the cruck frames by hand was not an easy job at Ben Law's Woodland House.

In this drawing it is possible to see how a naturally bent piece of sweet chestnut has been used as part of the design in Ben Law's house.

Round-wood pole roof at Hooke Park, Dorset; engineers: Buro Happold.

The interior of the grid-shell building at the Weald and Downland Museum of Ancient Buildings in Sussex, here being used for a green building fair; architects: Edward Cullinan, engineers: Buro Happold.

of laths that can be bolted together to create a grid shell. The best-known example of this is at the Weald and Downland Museum at Singleton in Sussex, which ably and elegantly demonstrates how large spaces can be spanned by structures using relatively small amounts of timber. In the spirit of using the valuable resource of timber as sparingly as possible, the strength of timber is used to great effect at Singleton, which forms the venue for a green building fair every year.

This method of building uses sophisticated metal connectors to join the laths together; this means that this is not a particularly inexpensive or natural form of building but one that may lead to other solutions

in the future. Sadly, other aspects of the building are less environmentally acceptable, such as the choice of foil-backed insulation. However, it is reasonable for a pioneering and experimental building not to try to tackle every problem at once.

A simpler form of grid-shell construction was used at Pishwanton in Scotland to create a much cheaper building. Designed by the architect Christopher Day and the engineer David Tasker, it was constructed by a local craftsman and volunteers. The oak laths once in place gain added strength from the sarking boards, which create a membrane across the grid. While spanning a smaller area than the Weald and Downland building, it demonstrates the use of a grid-shell

Detail of the grid-shell roof, showing oak laths and metal connectors; unfortunately, the insulating material behind is not natural.

An external view of the timber cladding and curving roof of the Singleton grid-shell building shows the expressive potential of this technology.

This building at Pishwanton also uses a much lower cost grid-shell, designed by David Tasker; it is strong enough to support a planted roof. (Photo: David Tasker)

in conjunction with other natural materials and building techniques and can be accomplished without the need for expensive, high-tech materials and connectors.

TIMBER CLADDING

An important decision in the design of any building is the choice of the external wall finish. The selection of certain finishes or a particular appearance may be a requirement for planning permission and there may be building regulation issues about fire safety. Timber cladding is popular with many natural builders as it reinforces the natural qualities of the building and can provide an inexpensive, low-maintenance and long-lasting solution. But it may not be possible in

every circumstance if there is no tradition of timber cladding in the area.

Timber rain screen cladding offers a wide range of aesthetic options and is frequently used in expensive, high-tech, urban buildings. Often such timber has not been sustainably sourced and is chosen more for its colour and style than the natural effects of the wood itself. There are several proprietary, composite wood products made from laminates with polymerized natural wood facings that appeal to designers who want a hi-tech finish. Timber boards in a more natural state can be painted, stained or oiled for protection or left to weather naturally.

Timber cladding usually consists of sawn boards that are fixed vertically or horizontally to battens with a ventilated cavity behind. Horizontal boards

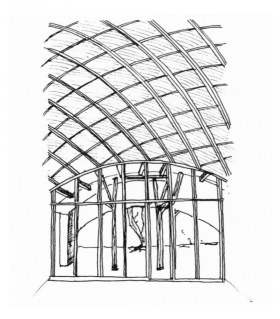

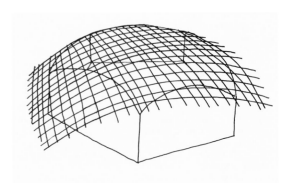

This diagram gives an indication of the form of the Pishwanton grid-shell.

A sketch of the interior space at Pishwanton.

Vertical timber boarding detail.

An alternative vertical timber boarding detail.

Vertical timber boarding at the Skelton Grange Environmental Education Centre in Leeds; architects: Leeds Environmental Design Associates (LEDA).

need to be arranged so that rain cannot easily get into the edge grain of the timber and vertical boards must have the end grain protected. There are various ways in which boards can be overlapped.

Boards can be used which retain a waney edge, reflecting the rough edge of the tree, usually with some of the bark showing, and a decision to do this is essentially stylistic. Boards can be fixed with nails, screws, secret fixings or even pegged or capped with wooden plugs. Depending on the chosen finishing treatment, different kinds of fixing can cause staining on the boards. Penetrating dampness that gets behind boards can also cause staining. The different details of timber cladding and the width of boards can make a significant difference to the appearance of a building. In some areas planners may request that boarding is used to mirror the local vernacular, where there is a tradition of boarded buildings.

Timber may be left untreated and allowed to weather down to what is normally a grey colour. Some timbers will blacken, especially if they are exposed to much dampness. There is now a range of environmentally friendly coatings for timber that are much better than previous synthetic paints and stains. Many are based on natural oils such as linseed, lemon and orange. They penetrate the wood much better, providing longer protection. Some protective

Horizontal timber boarding, designed by Andy Warren for a house in mid Wales.

Horizontal boarding with a waney edge on a straw-bale building, built by Jim Wallis in Gloucestershire.

Timber cladding to the unfired earth brick house in Perthshire; Arc Architects.

oils also contain a fine powder that provides ultra-violet light protection and helps the wood to retain its normal colour for longer. A wide range of stains is available, which will allow the wood to continue to breathe, and for its natural look not to be obscured.

BAMBOO

Bamboo should not really be in a chapter on timber since it is more like a grass than a tree; however, it could be a significant substitute for timber. Bamboo is one of the most natural and renewable materials available for building throughout the world, but it is barely exploited. There are thousands of species and some grow so fast that the growth can be seen by the naked eye. Thus bamboo can be cut and regenerated in a year or two. There are few examples of bamboo being used in buildings in the United Kingdom, but it has the potential to replace timber in many cases. Some bamboos can be used as structural members for large buildings and there have been experiments in South America in particular with both high-tech steel connectors and simpler methods of jointing bamboo members. Bamboo can also be used for roofs, gutters, flooring and cladding. Some companies in Europe are now marketing bamboo for building and even civil engineering structures such as bridges.

Bamboo is most familiar in the United Kingdom and Ireland as a replacement for wood in composite finished flooring products, but it is important to check which glues have been used in the composites. Bamboo can grow successfully in temperate climates, but a great deal more work is required before it becomes a commonplace material available to the natural builder. At present it is not readily available and would have to be imported from South America or Asia. Not a great deal is known about its durability in wet temperate climates but there are species that should be able to withstand British weather.

PROTECTING AGAINST DAMP AND ROT

Timber will last for a very long time if it is of good quality and allowed to dry out naturally when it gets wet. It does not need to be sealed against water, and paints and stains should allow the timber to breathe. Timber detailing is crucial to ensure that water is not allowed to collect on it but is easily shed. End grains

Timber post in metal post-holder.

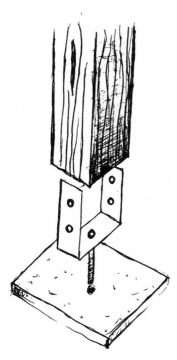

Timber metal post-holder.

Timber post sitting on stone or concrete plinth.

Hurdle making at the Inishowen Green Gathering; this hurdle was later plastered with hemp and lime.

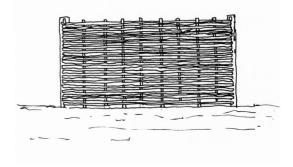

ABOVE: Hurdle made from hazel.

LEFT: Hurdle detail.

and other cut exposed areas should be protected. Timber posts should be supported off the ground in such a way that dampness cannot penetrate into the end grain. Galvanized steel shoes can be used or posts can be supported on stone or concrete plinths, provided that these allow water to run off and not sit at the bottom of the post.

HURDLES AND WATTLES

Hurdle and wattle making is an ancient craft and was used in early buildings with mud and dung (*see* Chapter 2). Timber crafts using hazel, willow and other timbers are making a comeback and there are hurdle makers who practise the skill and can teach others. Traditional laths are also being used in natural building in preference to plasterboard. Reed boards and reed matting are also used.

The use of hurdles for solar shading is becoming fashionable as an architectural motif and there are a number of modern buildings that have used natural materials in this way. An interesting example is the use of woven eucalyptus wood in cladding panels on the outside of a lion-viewing area at Whipsnade Zoo, designed by the architects Proctor and Matthews. In some cases the use of natural materials together with high-tech products can look incongruous, but it is very successful in this building.

Traditional lath construction; this would normally be plastered, but in this case has been left unplastered as it is so attractive in itself.

Eucalyptus hurdle used as solar shading on the lion house at Whipsnade Zoo; architects: Proctor and Matthews. (Photo: Tim Crocker)

Beautifully carved window details on cob building, designed by Ianto Evans; the roof edge detail could do with being a little more robust.

BELOW: Craftsman-made door from local timber at Cae Mabon.

CARVING, DOORS AND DETAILS

Another aspect of timber is its ability to impart a natural feeling to any building and the enormous scope it gives for artistic and sculptural expression. This is demonstrated particularly well at Cae Mabon in North Wales, where doors, entrances and windows reflect the natural qualities of wood. The potential for carving and decoration is endless though it is rarely used these days because of the dearth of craftsmen or the needs for speed and functionality.

LEFT: Carving over door at the Cae Mabon roundhouse in North Wales.

CHAPTER 4

Straw-Bale Building

WHAT IS STRAW-BALE BUILDING?

Straw has been used in building for thousands of years. It has been used as a binder mixed with clay and animal dung to create a form of walling (*see* Chapter 2). Straw-bale building, on the other hand, is a relatively modern form of construction that followed from the invention of the baling machine. Bales were used in the American prairies in the nineteenth and the early twentieth century when there was a shortage of timber and other building materials.

Straw bales should be regarded as a different material from loose straw and the two should not be confused. Anyone familiar with Lego can quickly grasp the concept of straw-bale building since the bales are like large building blocks. They can be arranged in a variety of ways to create a walling system that has been used to build quite sophisticated houses and in many other structures including roofs. Like most materials and methods discussed in this book, the bales are normally used in conjunction with other materials.

Reasons for Using Straw Bales

Straw-bale building readily meets the criteria for natural and ecological building. The straw comes from crops that are renewable and is a by-product rather than waste. Walls made of bales can have very good thermal and acoustic insulation properties. Anyone who has built a bale wall will soon find that the person helping on the other side of it cannot hear what you are saying. Bale walls look easy to construct and attract people who are looking for a form of construction that they think will be cheap and simple.

The thickness of the bales suggests that they will be quite inflexible in design, but it is possible to achieve a range of appearances. Bales can be laid on their sides or their backs, small and large bales can be used. They can be arranged in curves and circles. Some people are attracted by a rather uneven effect that can emulate traditional cob cottages and others have worked hard to disguise the unevenness of bales to fit in with a high-tech style.

Straw-bale building can be fun, especially if it involves a group of people in an exercise similar to barn raising. Some enthusiasts go further and see straw-bale building as an empowering experience, especially for women, 'It is woman-friendly, joyful, optimistic and highly motivated', according to

Straw bales for sale in a County Down field; sometimes straw is plentiful and sometimes not, depending on the weather and the harvest.

Wall raising is an enjoyable community effort, as here at a school classroom in Ireland, but keeping the enthusiasm going during the boring bits is harder.

Barbara Jones. In fact, most forms of self-build experience are good for people's self-esteem and confidence and the use of bales has no particular magical properties in this regard. The quality of the experience depends more on how well the project is organized. Some straw-bale enthusiasts promote the idea that this form of building can be done by amateurs and that therefore little expertise is required, and, because of the many books and Internet sites about it, it is easy to think that you can teach yourself; but as a result some straw buildings in the United Kingdom have been quite poorly designed and badly constructed since little expert help was involved. As with any other form of building, it is important to get good design and professional help. In particular, structural issues must be carefully considered.

Dangers of 'Bale Frenzy'

This is a term usually used to describe the overenthusiastic and careless placing of bales during construction, but it also represents an attitude of mind in which some people become blind to other aspects of building. Often the decision to use this material is based on impulse rather than a careful analysis as to whether it is the most appropriate. Many of those who have approached us for advice about straw-bale building have decided on this form of construction

even before they have a site. Our normal advice is to start at the beginning by thinking carefully about what they want to do and why, and only decide what material to use once things have advanced a little further and designs are being prepared. However, for many people, the decision to use straw bale is almost like a religious conversion. Catherine Wanek, editor of *The Last Straw* journal, indeed, describes strawbalers as 'converts' (Wanek, in Kennedy, *Art of Natural Building*, 2002). In my view, this is not a sound or rational basis for choosing a building material, since it is not holistic in approach. One straw-bale building in Ireland has uPVC windows, for instance.

The reason for this impulsive commitment to straw is the way that it has been portrayed as the ultimate solution to 'cheap', environmentally friendly building. This is reinforced by the fact that, when there is a glut of bales, they can be bought for less than £1 each. At other times, however, straw can be quite expensive and in short supply. In many places straw is used in large quantities for mushroom composting and is also burned in small power stations. As will be explained below, straw-bale buildings are rarely cheaper than the conventional, particularly if they are built properly. Where claims are made that straw buildings are cheap this is because labour costs have been reduced due to self-building or the

Straw-bale buildings are found all over the world; this house designed by the architect Andy Horn in South Africa is plastered with an earth plaster from earth found on the site.

work of volunteers. The additional thickness of the walls leads to other aspects of the building being more expensive.

Problems with Using Straw Bales

Bales, by their nature, are not bought in builders' merchants and are rarely prepared for construction. This means that they can be unpredictable in size, shape, baling-twine tension and moisture content. All of these can be controlled, but not if the bales come straight off the field on to the building site. As straw is an organic material, it is subject to rot in damp conditions; the question of moisture is discussed below. Plastering the walls can be expensive and hard work, and the wall plate, footing, window and door details are more complicated than in a conventional building. Many people assume that a straw-bale buildings can be a fire hazard, but, in fact, they are no more risky than any other building material if constructed properly. Mice and other rodents, even nesting birds, on the other hand are dismissed as an issue in most of the books on straw bale, but in my experience they can be a small problem. In one straw-bale building, that we built, the mice were running around on the wall plate as we were building; they came with the bales from the farmer's barn! Rodents can create problems by creating runs and nests within the walls. This is only stopped when the walls are plastered, but this cannot necessarily be done right away.

As with any other material discussed here, the pros and cons of bale building have to be considered and a careful decision taken as to whether they are appropriate. In my opinion, this type of building is most appropriate for self-building, with plenty of volunteer help, both for housing, outbuildings and some community and agricultural projects. Bales are unlikely to be used for urban mass housing, but they can be used in educational and commercial buildings. Straw bales provide an effective way to achieve high levels of insulation and, if you can cope with the thick walls, it may be the ideal solution. Bales have

73

been used in high-tech buildings such as business parks; there is such a project at Hewish in North Somerset, where the developer/farmers Chris and Simon Redding have constructed Grange Office Park. They have built walls using 2m-long bales (2m × 1m × 1m) to create very low-energy offices. The development also features rainwater harvesting and an on-site biodigester sewage scheme.

DIFFERENT FORMS OF CONSTRUCTION WITH BALES

Nebraska-Style Load-Bearing Walls

It is possible to build straw-bale walls that are free-standing and self-supporting, They are strong enough to carry the weight of roofs and can even be built to two or three storeys, although this is uncommon. A qualified structural engineer should be involved in the design of most straw-bale buildings,

and especially where the walls are load-bearing. A great deal of work on structural properties has been done in the western USA, where local building regulations require structural calculations on even the smallest building because of the earthquake risk.

Load-bearing walls require the bales to be stacked, usually in a stretcher bond (with the walls well tied in to other walls at corners). It is important to avoid unsupported ends of walls, but rectangular and circular buildings can be constructed. The bales need to be fixed to the ground to stabilize their position and then pinned together to prevent their moving around during construction. Bales can be laid on their backs or on edge, but are stronger on their backs. A key feature of construction is the wall plate, which transfers the weight of the roof on to the bales and also ties the bale walls together. Wall-plate design is a crucial aspect of straw-bale construction and must evenly distribute roof loads.

Large, three string bales used for eco-offices at Hewish, Somerset; architects: White Design. (Photo: White Design)

Load-bearing, straw-bale walls, where the bales have to be pinned and stacked in stretcher bond; the wall plate is tied to the ground in such a way that the bales are compressed.

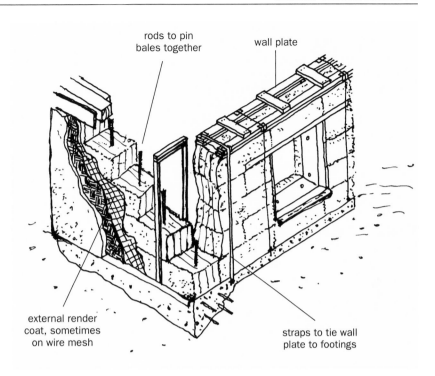

rods to pin bales together

wall plate

external render coat, sometimes on wire mesh

straps to tie wall plate to footings

BELOW: Diagrammatic section showing pinning and tying down the wall plate to foundations (foundation detail not shown here).

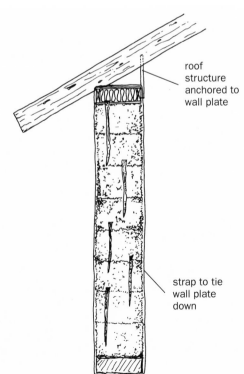

roof structure anchored to wall plate

strap to tie wall plate down

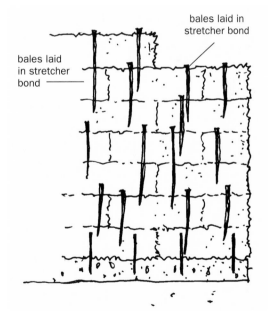

bales laid in stretcher bond

bales laid in stretcher bond

It is normal practice to pin the bales with hazel sticks or staves; in the past steel rods were used, however, this is a difficult task and external pinning is probably better and easier.

Straw-bale wall showing the wall plate and nylon packaging strapping to tie the wall to the foundations; there is a limit to the tension on this kind of strapping and some straw-balers have even used the strapping from 44-tonne trucks.

Pinning the bales is a difficult part of bale construction. Early American literature recommended banging steel reinforcing rods through them, but this then changed to wooden staves or bamboo. It is not always easy to pin the bales, especially if the straw is tightly packed and the pins can easily go out of line. More recently, research in the USA has shown that much of the structural stress in bale walls is taken on the outer skin and external pinning has been suggested. The pins, usually of bamboo rod, have to be fixed to the outside of the bales and tied through them. This is also not always an easy job. The wall plate must also be pinned to the straw walls.

In order to use stretcher bond with the bales it will be necessary to make special half bales, and these need to be restrung from a full bale and then cut. Special bale needles have been developed to facilitate this. Some sources recommend the use of loose straw to pack out any left over spaces, such as on the wall plate, and others have suggested the use of mud and straw to fill up any gaps for air-tightness and better insulation. In the humid British and Irish climate, it is not a good idea to introduce any wet materials into the wall and the use of loose straw should also be avoided since it is a fire risk. It is best to get the bales to fit as tightly as possible.

Frame Construction

Instead of relying on straw-bale walls to support the roof, it is possible to create some kind of frame construction and to fill between the frame with bales. There are a number of options for this and bales can be used with a wide variety of different kinds of frame. Frames of steel and concrete have been used as well as timber. Bales are laid in much the same way as in load-bearing construction between any vertical supports. They need to be pinned together and fixed to the columns and beams. The bale wall section must be structurally cohesive, and even if it is not taking the load from the roof it must be able to withstand wind and shear forces and not be free to move independently of the main structure.

An example of a modern, relatively conventional frame building of steel and concrete but which uses straw-bale infill may be seen at the University of the West of England. At opposite ends of the building on the staircase walls, prefabricated straw-bale infill panels have been inserted into a steel frame. A test panel was initially constructed and tested for weathering and structural properties (*see* picture on page 78). The panel was subjected to a number of structural tests including it being pushed over.

Without a small 'truth window' inside, the uninformed would not be aware that these walls are made of straw-bale. Originally it had been hoped to have more of the walls made in this way but the project was restricted to a small experiment, which has been monitored. This showed how a relatively large public building could use straw-bales instead of concrete, brick or proprietary cladding systems. Based on this experience, the architects White Design have gone on to use straw bales in other projects, such as the business park at Hewish described earlier and buildings constructed in Wales and York.

Other Post and Beam Methods

Straw-bale infill can be used with timber post and beam construction methods. The timber posts may be highly finished, rectangular in form, or round-wood poles can be used. These are aesthetic and sustainability decisions rather than structural ones. The timber can be kiln-dried or green straight out of the forest. Straw bales are suitable to use with green and round-wood timber since the bales can flex and may be able to accommodate some movement in the wood as it dries.

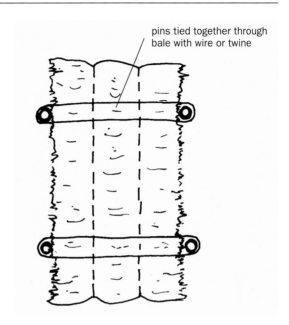

pins tied together through bale with wire or twine

Plan of a bale, showing external pinning; ties must be threaded through the bales, which is time-consuming, but the compression is largely taken on the rendered skin, so the pins are helping to reinforce this.

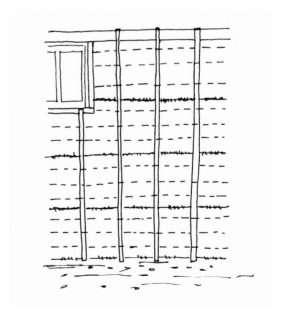

Elevation of external pinning.

77

Engineering tests on a straw-bale panel designed by White Design Architects, for the School of Architecture building at the University of the West of England. (Photo: White Design)

A highly practical approach to frame construction is to use composite timber I-beams as the uprights; these can be sized to the width of a bale and the bales inserted between each upright, but the spacing of timber uprights will depend very much on the design and structural calculations.

The interplay between timber frame and straw-bale infill provides a wide range of aesthetic and structural options. If there are concerns about the ability of straw to be durable, the use of a timber frame provides assurance that the building will not fall down, and the bales can be taken out and replaced, if necessary. The flexibility of straw-bale construction and the variety of approaches and solutions that are feasible can be seen in a house built in Herefordshire (*see* pictures on pages 81 and 82) in

Gable end of the University of the West of England building in Bristol; the blue and orange squares are straw-bale panels.

which the ground floor walls are built with straw-bale infill in a timber stud frame wall, whereas the upper frame structure provided a platform off which the upper floor bales could be placed without a frame (*see* drawing on page 82). This illustrates neatly the variety of possibilities with bales, provided that structural integrity is retained.

The apparent advantage of load-bearing construction is the need for less timber, but the difference between load-bearing and timber-frame infill is marginal. Nebraska-style, load-bearing walls may be a more purist solution but may not be appropriate in many cases.

In Ben Law's Woodland House the straw bales are used as a form of infill insulation, placed after the external cladding and main structure was in place. This has advantages over loose-quilt insulation because bales are rigid and can be easily lifted into place and there is no risk that the insulation will slump in the cavity.

DETAILING STRAW-BALE BUILDINGS

There are a number of key issues to be borne in mind when designing and building a straw-bale building that are not encountered with conventional buildings. First of all, the width of the wall is much greater than in most other building types (except cob). The wall plate has to be wide and is part of the structure.

Barry House in Somerset, semi-permanent, timber-frame, low-impact, straw-bale building that also uses cordwood gable walls; the timber frame is supported on tyre foundations.

Tyre foundation detail for temporary straw-bale buildings.

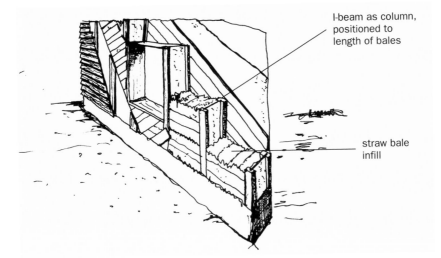

I-beam as column, positioned to length of bales

straw bale infill

Timber frame using I-beams with straw-bale infill; the straw is not taking any load in this form of construction and could be removed without the building needing to be taken down in the future.

Straw-bale building in County Waterford, where straw has been used as an infill with a timber frame.

Self-built, straw-bale house in Herefordshire, finished with a lime render.

The heads of the wall must be tied together and the roof structure designed to brace the walls so that they will not move in or out. A further point to remember with load-bearing walls is that the bales will compress if there is a heavy roof, and this means that the wall will settle and the wall plate and roof structure will move down. It is best to leave the plastering of the walls until this settlement has finished or to use a lightweight roof.

Window and door openings will also be affected by the settlement and thus the heads must allow for this downward movement. This problem does not occur in frame buildings. One solution is to provide wedge-shaped packers that can be knocked out above the door or window head. The window and door openings need to be formed by a box that fits into the wall; these are best constructed first so that the bales can be packed in tightly around them. This is one

area where straw-bale building becomes a little more expensive, as much timber goes into the wall plate and openings.

Detailing around window openings is important since bales below the sill are particularly vulnerable to rain penetration. A good weatherproof sill should be incorporated into the walls, which can throw rain well away from the walls.

Wall Plate and Strapping

The design of the wall plate is crucial for load-bearing, straw-bale buildings, and, in particular, it must be firmly tied to the foundations of the building. The roof must also be fixed to the wall plate to comply with the building regulations, but straps on to the straw walls are not the answer. There are a number of possible details and methods for doing this, but the main principle is to tie the wall plate

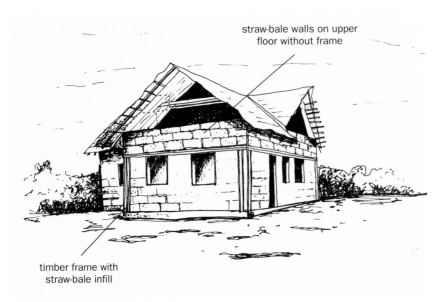

straw-bale walls on upper
floor without frame

timber frame with
straw-bale infill

The Herefordshire house is a hybrid form of construction with timber frame to the ground floor creating a first-floor platform off which the first-floor bales were constructed.

Ben Law's Woodland House in Sussex, where straw bales have been used for insulation; they are plastered internally with earth but there is a timber rain screen cladding externally. (Photo: Stephen F. Morley)

82

and thus any connection to the roof direct to the foundations. This can be done with nylon packaging strapping, but there are limits to the tension to which this can be set. One expert uses haulage straps from trucks, which can be tensioned to a much higher strain.

INSULATING PROPERTIES OF STRAW-BALE WALLS

One of the main reasons for using straw-bale walls is that they should provide a high standard of insulation, thus substantially reducing energy usage and carbon emissions. Despite the fact that a great deal of research has been done in the USA on straw-bale building, there is still much disagreement about the standards of insulation that can be achieved. Research in the USA suggests that the R-value (thermal resistance) for a straw-bale wall, built according to Arizona structural codes, is $2.8W/m^2K$. This gives a thermal transmission value of $0.35W/m^2K$. Myrhmann and MacDonald give an R-value of 2.5 to 3. The Building Research Establishment in Scotland, in a study for Community Self Build Scotland, gave a figure of $0.11W/m^2K$ for a 600mm-thick bale wall with a rain-screen cladding. Barbara Jones quotes a range of figures varying from 0.13 to 0.31; she says that bales of 450mm width have a U value of 0.13; Borer and Harris say 0.2.

The range of thermal insulation values given in the literature varies substantially. This is not helped by the use of a wide range of different ways of presenting the figures (the Americans still use imperial units, for instance). The main conclusion is to be careful about accepting exaggerated claims of thermal performance. As in other building types, the theoretical performance can be affected by moisture content, robustness of details and construction, cold bridging and so on. More carefully controlled scientific studies are needed to confirm insulation performance, but straw bale should still hold its own against many other forms of construction. As with other forms of natural building, hard and fast figures are not available from official-looking documents such as Agrément certificates, and thus it is necessary to go back to first principles when calculating predicted energy performance.

Window-box frame made of plywood built into the straw-bale wall as the bales are raised; they must be pinned into the bales, the window is added later.

This window sill detail at the Herefordshire straw-bale house is not ideal since it was a charming afterthought; a more substantial sill with an overhang would be better.

Foundations

In frame construction, the bale walls can be built off a timber platform suspended above the ground. Load-bearing walls, however, are likely to be built off foundations that transmit the load direct to the ground. A number of possible foundation details can be used, but it is important to ensure that there is always protection from dampness as explained below.

Shaping the Bales

It is possible to trim the bales, once they have been erected, with a chainsaw to create curved and angled shapes. For many this is one of the most attractive features of straw-bale construction, since these sculptural qualities can be produced in the plasterwork.

Care has to be taken not to cut through the baling twine. Straight and curved walls can be created, but it is important not to forget that bales are rectangular when designing a straw-bale building.

It is also useful to tidy up the bales before the plastering and this can be done by hand with shears or with a strimmer. The edges of the bales are a perfectly good key for any plaster and it should not be necessary to use any wire or stucco mesh. However, where there are complicated details and edges where there is a junction, it is sometimes necessary to use expanded metal mesh to control cracking. Tying the mesh into the bales is a most unpleasant job and so the detailing should be done carefully to avoid the need for this.

Straw-bale wall supported on a timber platform built off a stone plinth and footing; this is suitable only for a temporary building and may not be acceptable to the building control office.

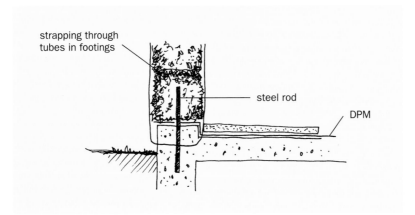

strapping through tubes in footings

steel rod

DPM

Straw-bale wall built off a conventional concrete footing but with an upstand.

Circular straw-bale building in County Monaghan, Ireland, built by Marcus McCabe, with thatched roof.

PROTECTING AGAINST DAMP

Straw will rot if it is allowed to get too wet and thus the detailing must ensure that driving rain does not get on to the walls or be allowed to soak in anywhere. Ideally, any roof should have a generous overhang or, even better, a veranda to minimize the amount of rain getting on to the walls. Any ends of walls and openings must be especially well detailed and sills are particularly vulnerable if the window is deeply recessed. The foot of the walls and the foundations are a controversial area, since many building control officials will expect to see a normal damp-proof course there. Rising damp is a questionable concept and not the main issue with straw. For straw-bale walls a conventional damp-proof course (DPC) can be a problem, allowing moisture to collect at the bottom of the bales on top of the plastic. In a well-built and well-plastered straw-bale wall, this should not be too much of a problem, but where moisture readings have been taken, the dampness is greater towards the foot of the wall. Instead, the ideal footing details should allow water to drain away. Where the bale walls sit on a timber platform there should be a reasonable projection, allowing water to drain away from the platform.

But if straw-bale walls do get wet, natural materials can have the ability to dry out and recover. The best way this can happen is through natural drying from the sun. However, this means that there may be problems on north-facing walls or in areas where there is overshadowing from trees or other buildings. If some bales do get wet from a plumbing or roof leak then they will start to rot, but they can be pulled out and replaced. This was done successfully on a

Straw-bales that have started to rot due to a roof leak; however, they were pulled out and replaced without difficulty, although the roof had to be propped since the wall was load-bearing; the spores that grow on damp straw are dangerous, causing an illness known as 'farmer's lung'.

building in Northern Ireland. It is important also to cover bales so that they do not get soaked during construction.

For this reason, for anyone who is anxious about the longevity of straw buildings, the frame solution is the best because if there are any problems with the bales they can easily be replaced without compromising the structure of the whole. There are much

quoted examples of straw-bale buildings that have lasted over a hundred years, but these are in relatively hot, dry climates. In the United Kingdom and Ireland, where humidity levels are high and driving, almost horizontal, rain is common, we have to be sure that dampness is not a problem.

In a study carried out by the University of Plymouth (Goodhew *et al.*) of a five-year-old, framed, straw-bale building in Devon, some localized damp areas of straw were found where the moisture level was 25 to 27 per cent. This was caused by wind-driven rain penetrating the external render, but other parts of the wall remained quite dry. It is generally agreed that straw will start to degrade at 20 per cent moisture content, so it is a matter of some concern if moisture levels above this are found. The Plymouth study raised many questions about issues such as how quickly moisture is dissipated from wet plastering, and how the moisture seemed to increase with higher temperatures and thus higher humidity. Insufficient scientific studies have been done to monitor straw-bale buildings over time in the United Kingdom, but some work has been done in the USA and can be downloaded from the Ecological Building Network website. As a rule of thumb, moisture levels should remain at or below 14 to 15 per cent, and anyone building a straw building would be well advised to insert a number of probes that allow the moisture level to be monitored.

Bales straight off the field may be quite damp, especially if harvested in a wet autumn. It is then better to use bales from the previous season that have been well air-dried in a barn. This can involve planning well ahead so that bales can be obtained in the autumn harvest but then carefully stored and dried over the winter away from any rain, to be used for building in the summer months. Bales should be kept dry during construction and, since it rains in the summer as well as winter, this can involve the tedious job of covering the whole building with tarpaulins every night. In a few cases, straw buildings have been constructed under a temporary shelter to provide weather protection; this is particularly necessary if volunteers or a community are involved. Frame buildings where the roof can go on at an early stage provide another solution to protection from the rain during construction.

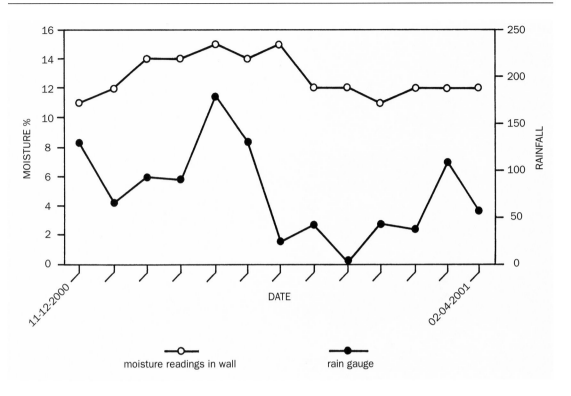

Example of moisture readings taken in straw-bale building in Devon by Goodhew et al., showing how moisture levels remain reasonably steady but follow rainfall to some extent. (Courtesy: Elsevier-Science Direct)

EXTERNAL FINISHES

For many years American straw-bale buildings were plastered with cement. This was usually sprayed on to the walls, sometimes with a product called 'gunnite', which is a synthetic fibrous cement product. Many straw-bale walls were covered in a stucco metal mesh that helped to prevent cracking and provide a key for the render. In the United Kingdom most straw-bale buildings have been plastered with lime (*see* Chapter 6). Lime renders have a greater flexibility, are softer and will work better with straw bales; however, they can also be expensive and great care must be taken in how they are applied. The final finish can be a lime wash, which can then be painted or self-coloured. We have mixed in linseed oil with the lime wash, which has ensured a greater protection against rain. The use of linseed oil is controversial, however, as some suggest that this reduces the breathability of the wall.

A high-tech solution to cladding straw-bale walls has been used in London where the architects Wigglesworth and Till have use a ventilated rain screen of galvanized steel cladding and corrugated polycarbonate sheets. The cladding is sealed against rodents and insects with a perforated ventilating strip top and bottom. Part of the sheeting is clear so that the straw can clearly be seen behind. While this is a novel solution in a secluded garden, it might not work where there could be danger from vandals. Another option is to use earth plasters and there are examples of this in the United Kingdom and Europe. Internally, earth plasters should be fine and trouble-free, but earth plasters have not been fully tested externally in a rainy environment. A Scandinavian straw-bale house that I stayed in had earth plaster external walls and these failed and had to be replaced by lime.

The classroom in Ireland, shown under construction on page 72, plastered with lime and linseed oil.

External polycarbonate and corrugated rain screen cladding to a straw-bale wall for a house in Islington, north London: architects: Sarah Wigglesworth and Jeremy Till.

STRAW-BALE BUILDINGS WHERE THE BALES ARE HIDDEN

There are a number of straw-bale buildings where it is not immediately obvious that bales have been used. Some people want to express the bales and others want to hide them. Where bales are being used purely for their insulation then it is possible to clad them internally and externally with a variety of materials.

OPPOSITE: Self-coloured lime plaster used on the Waterford straw-bale house; the lime render can give a soft appearance without sharp edges, if this is the aesthetic required.

This has been done in another house in Hereford-shire (*see* picture on page 121), where the external walls are timber-clad and internally a board has been used which is plastered. Thus, apart from the great thickness of the walls, it would not be obvious that this is a straw-bale building. The occupant in this case was aiming for a high degree of energy efficiency, both in insulation and air-tightness and this has been achieved creating an almost zero-energy house. The walls are clad with locally-harvested larch or Douglas fir. It is important that there is an air gap between the bales and the timber. The timber acts as a rain screen and the bales should stay dry. There is an interesting debate about whether a combination of timber-cladding and straw-bale can produce a very airtight

A timber-clad, straw-bale building in West Wales, designed by Andy Warren; this house is so energy-efficient that passive solar gain from the conservatory is the main source of energy and the house requires little heating; the north side is rendered with lime.

and energy-efficient building or whether a plastered building would be better. Nick Grant, a member of the Association of Environment Conscious Builders (AECB), subjected this timber-clad, straw-bale building in Herefordshire to an air-tightness test, with very good results; details of this may be accessed through the AECB website.

It is important when the bales are clad inside and out to ensure that there is no possibility of dampness getting to them, since any rot might not be detected for years. Furthermore, there might be a risk of interstitial condensation where high humidity levels could result in moisture condensing on a surface that could come into contact with the bales. In the case of the

Grant house, the walls can breathe, thus allowing vapour to permeate through them. Breather membranes have been used. Another straw-bale house in Wales, designed by Andy Warren, has timber cladding on some walls and is heated largely by passive solar gain.

FIRE PROTECTION

A great deal of research has been done in the USA and elsewhere on the fire performance of straw-bale walls. Where bales are fully covered in a lime or cement plaster on both sides, the fire performance is claimed to be extremely good. Many conventional

A straw-bale building, destroyed by fire, at Carrickfergus Urban Farm; the vandals had several attempts to burn down the building before they were successful and, as can be seen, the straw has not burned whereas the timber is badly charred.

materials will perform much more poorly and rely heavily on toxic fire-retardant chemicals to protect them. Since the bales are dense and there is little oxygen within the walls, bales char in a fire, in a similar way to wood. With the addition of a plaster, most straw walls can withstand fire for some time. Unfortunately, few fire brigades are aware of this and, where fires have occurred in straw-bale buildings, the fire brigade have a tendency to push and prod at the walls, breaking them up, thus exposing loose straw to the fire. Even where this has happened, it can be seen that little of the straw has burned as in the picture (*right*) of a burnt-out straw-bale building. But the timber has been badly destroyed. It would be beneficial to arrange for the local fire brigade to visit straw buildings and to run a seminar for the crews showing videos from the USA of fire tests. It is also important to take great care during construction. Loose straw should not be left lying around on the floor but should be swept up regularly and kept well away from the site.

A straw-bale building under construction where loose straw has been left lying around; this can be a fire hazard since tightly packed straw will not burn but loose will.

BALES IN ROOFS AND FLOORS

Some straw-bale buildings have used bales as roof insulation, inside the roof structure. Technically this is feasible but it can lead to problems since the bales usually remain unplastered and exposed to rodent attack and fire. The normal solution is to use one of the natural insulation materials discussed in Chapter 11. Others have experimented with placing straw bales on to the ground and then casting a concrete floor slab on top and around the bales. This is also a risky strategy and not to be recommended because the bales could become damp and rot, leaving voids underneath the concrete. The bales have also been used between the floor joists in a suspended timber floor, but this is also a fire risk since the bales cannot be plastered.

HAY BALES

Some people refer to straw-bale buildings as 'hay-bale buildings'. Normally, wheat and barley straw are used for the bales and hay is not really suitable. Hay is a good source of food but has been used for building only where no straw was available. It is also not suitable for people who suffer from hay fever. Other materials such as hemp and flax straw have been used, but they are not as easy to work with as wheat or barley.

SERVICES

It is best to design straw-bale buildings so that wet services do not run through or inside the walls. If there is a leak then water can soak into the walls for some time before it is noticed. Electrical services, on

Bedroom in a straw-bale house in Herefordshire.

the other hand, can be ducted through the walls. Wooden spikes can be inserted as grounds for electrical sockets if necessary. Straw walls can even be chased for service ducts, but this should be avoided if at all possible.

STRAW-BALE INTERIORS

The interiors of straw-bale buildings can reflect the uneven nature of the straw-bale walls with uneven plaster or can be finished to provide conventional, smooth walls. Many such buildings include a truth window that leaves a small section of straw exposed so that it can be seen that the straw is there. Straw-bale buildings can have a different character from

OPPOSITE: A hay bale temporary building at the 2005 Inishowen Green Gathering in Donegal; this building was an effective seminar room with the projector being powered by a small wind turbine; note the No Smoking sign.

other buildings because of the thickness of the walls and the potential sculptural characteristics that the bales possess.

THE POTENTIAL OF STRAW-BALE

An effort has been made here to give a balanced view of the pros and cons of straw-bale construction. Those converts to this form of construction tend only to emphasize the advantages and will not necessarily be pleased that some of its shortcomings have been mentioned. However, anyone embarking on such a novel form of construction should be aware of the potential problems and ensure that proper steps are taken to design and build the building to the highest possible standard. In the right situation, bales can meet many of the needs of the natural builder, offering insulation, wall thickness and an economical solution.

It is important if you want to use straw bales in your building that you should get some hands-on

ABOVE: *Living room in the Waterford straw-bale house, with a contrast between the lime-plastered, rounded, straw-bale walls and the timber posts and beams.*

Interior of the conservatory in the West Wales straw-bale building – see also *the photograph of this house on page 90.*

Straw-bale walls of the conference room at the Centre for Alternative Technology in Wales.

experience of building with them. Several people run courses and invite volunteers to help with construction. You can then tell whether it suits you or not. This is as important for architects and builders as it is for self-builders. It is important to get knowledgeable, professional help in designing the building, and, when a scheme is prepared, it must be designed to incorporate the straw bales at an early stage. The dimensions of the building must be based on the bale module, and openings and structure arranged to fit in with this. A structural engineer should be consulted for all but the simplest of single-storey buildings to ensure that proper bracing will be provided and that any loads can be carried. Openings and other details should be arranged to minimize the cutting of bales.

CHAPTER 5

Green and Natural Roofs

WHAT ARE GREEN AND NATURAL ROOFS?

For the potential natural builder, roofing is one of the most problematic subjects. Many of the natural walling and building methods described here require a good 'hat' to protect the material from heavy rain, and thus the roof is a crucial aspect of design. However, the creation of a reliable and waterproof roof often involves the use of natural materials that are usually quite expensive. A less costly roof will inevitably be made from synthetic and non-natural materials. As with other aspects of natural building, a pragmatic compromise may be necessary.

Many buildings are described as having a 'green roof' in consequence of looking green because of the grass or other natural vegetation on the top. Such a roof is referred to here as a 'planted roof'. These are often built up with a range of synthetic, petrochemical-based materials that undermine the environmental claims for 'green roofs'. In this case it is necessary to select those materials which are the least damaging to the environment. However, the use of synthetic materials may be justified because of the other benefits of planted roofs.

Genuinely natural roofs are usually made from timber and covered with natural slates, stones or timber. However, even with such roofs a synthetic breathable roofing felt may be used under the outer surface, thus slightly compromising the natural characteristics. Really natural roofs are made from thatch, timber or other natural and renewable materials and these are largely found on traditional and historic buildings that have been renovated or restored. Despite the cost and skills involved in creating thatched and other natural roofs, some natural builders will opt for this solution in order to avoid the use of synthetic and petrochemical-based products.

THATCH

Thatch is, in many ways, one of the most natural and greenest materials dealt with in this book. It has been used for centuries and the technology is still alive today, with a recent growth in the number of skilled thatchers because thatch is now being selected for new buildings as well as the repair of old ones. Thatch can be made from wetland reeds and many of these are imported from eastern Europe; it is also possible to source reeds more locally, though not without difficulty. Reeds play an important role in helping to clean up pollutants and providing important habitats for birds and other wildlife, and reed beds are now also increasingly used as part of sewage treatment. Long straw was also used extensively in thatching, but it has to be specially grown. Most modern agricultural practices mean that normal straw is too short and it may also be weakened by fertilizers and pesticides. Barley and oat straw does not last as long as wheat straw; reeds can have a life of twenty-five years, rushes and grasses last for only a few. The list below summarizes the materials that can be used:

Thatched roof at the Cae Mabon roundhouse in North Wales, showing the expressive forms that can be achieved with thatch.

- broom
- heather
- rushes
- marram grass
- flax
- water reed
- wheat 'reed'
- wheat straw
- barley straw
- oat straw.

There are many forms of thatch, different materials have been used and different styles and techniques employed in different regions. Thatch requires a great degree of skill and experience for it to be used properly, and, because it is labour intensive, it is reasonably expensive as a form of roofing. Properly experienced thatchers are more easily found in areas where thatch has been traditional such as Norfolk, Leicestershire and Rutland, where there has been a need to restore historic buildings.

Thatched roofs will provide a reasonable amount of insulation but are not fully air-tight, and additional insulation and energy-efficiency measures will be necessary if a very low-energy building is required. Some modern buildings with thatched roofs do not have authentic thatch because a conventional roof has been constructed and then thatch laid as a cosmetic adornment on top. Thatch can also look very beautiful internally, but this is only suitable for situations that do not require building control approval. Reed mats are available from eco builders' merchants and these have been used on ceilings; this would normally present problems in terms of the applicability of fire regulations.

The bulk of the literature and advice about thatch is concerned with vernacular building and the restoration of old buildings, but there are some good sources of information on thatching. For a time there was a great deal of prejudice against thatch and this affected the ability of homeowners to get affordable insurance, but this problem seems to have eased recently. On the other hand, thatched roofs may fall foul of building regulations concerned with fire, and permission to install them may be refused by local authorities; new buildings in which thatch is proposed that are close to adjoining properties or to roads may run into difficulties in getting approval. There are measures that can be used to reduce fire dangers, however; internal fire barriers can be installed and the thatch can be sprayed with flame-retardant chemicals. Another measure is to install a ridge water-drenching pipe with an easily accessible stop valve.

Thatched roofs are sometimes covered with wire mesh to restrict birds and vermin. Sometimes this is just done to the ridge and gables. Clearly, for the natural builder the addition of toxic flame retardants and similar measures may dim an enthusiasm for thatch, but, despite this, new thatched buildings are still being constructed.

There are many techniques of thatching with their own extensive terminology, which varies from place to place. In summary, the straw or reeds are collected into bundles; the bundles must be drawn or pulled to remove short straws and any unnecessary material. The bundles are fixed to the roof with hazel 'scallops', 'skivers' or 'sways'. These unfamiliar terms vary from place to place. Cramps made out of hazel bent into a hairpin shape are used to secure a 'band'. Mild steel rods and spikes are also used and thatching nails provide fixings to battens. Modern thatching may

Thatch can be seen on the underside of this roof because it is a small meditation room/summer house in a back garden.

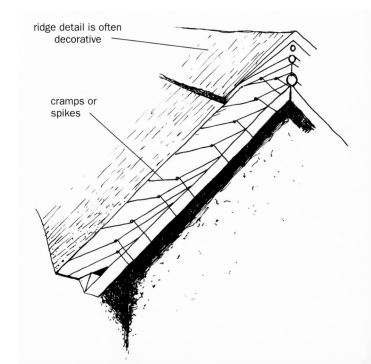

ridge detail is often decorative

cramps or spikes

Section through a thatched roof, showing the way in which cramps or spikes are used.

Thatched summer house or meditation room in an Oxford back garden, built with cob walls and a thatched roof by Michael Buck.

include securing bundles of reeds with polypropylene twine. The ragged ends of the bundles are trimmed and there is a wide range of traditional tools used to give the final, neat appearance.

The roof ridge, overhangs, gables and hips can be made in a variety of ways, which gives local character to thatching techniques. In cost terms, thatch is comparable to costly good quality, natural slates, perhaps twice as expensive as shingles and three times the cost of clay pantiles. Examples of thatched roofs are shown in other chapters, where natural builders have used thatch with earth or straw buildings.

TIMBER ROOFS, BOARDS AND SHINGLES AND SHAKES

Probably the most accessible and affordable solution

to a natural roof is to use timber. Traditionally, shingles are the most common material and these are like small slates, cut from a range of woods, which are nailed to the roof in much the same way as tiles or slates. To obtain shingles is not difficult today as there is a wide range of suppliers with imported products. But there are also woodworkers who are making shingles for sale or to special order at a local level if suitable wood is available.

Western red cedar shingles are made in Canada and the USA and are imported by a wide range of timber merchants and suppliers in the United Kingdom. The principal source is British Columbia. Some western red cedar is home-grown but it is not common in the United Kingdom and Ireland. Most of the imported cedar is not FSC-certified and thus the management of the forests concerned must be

Western Red Cedar shingles were used for the Kindersley Centre in Berkshire.

Nailing sweet chestnut shingles to the roof of Ben Law's Woodland House. (Photo: Stephen F. Morley)

Welsh-made redwood shingles at Cae Mabon.

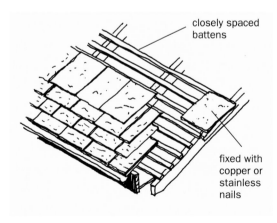

closely spaced battens

fixed with copper or stainless nails

Shingles require a substantial overlap and closely-spaced battens.

questioned. The handful of sawmills in North America which do claim to have FSC chain of custody cannot keep up with demand. Western red cedar has become very fashionable with architects in recent years and is used for roofing and cladding, often on buildings that are claimed to be environmentally friendly with a vague assertion that the wood is from well-managed forests.

Other timbers may be used, such as redwood or chestnut. The timber must be of good quality otherwise the shingles will warp and soon twist. The pitch of the roof must be sufficient to cast off the rain as quickly as possible, but inevitably the constant wetting and drying may lead to some decay over time. Shingle roofs may have to be renewed more frequently than tiles or slates.

102

Timber-boarded roof at the Centre for Alternative Technology, Wales.

Shingles are very attractive, but the wood will darken with weathering. Many shingles are needed for even a small building. Ben Law's relatively small house required 12,000 sweet chestnut shingles; each had to be pre-drilled and attached with copper clout nails to conventional battens (the roof was covered with a synthetic breather membrane first). Getting shingles made from a local forest may seem like a romantic option, but it is possible to do this in some parts of the country.

Boarded Roofs

Another timber roof option is a detail borrowed from Scandinavia in which overlapping boards are laid vertically down the roof or the roof is boarded and then smaller capping battens are fixed over the joints. This solution can look quite attractive at first but the boards can twist and start to decay. It is a roofing solution that may require frequent attention or replacement after a number of years. The fixing details are important, and battens should be placed close together to restrict any movement in the timber.

A house in Hackney in London has been built with a cedar-boarded roof that is wrapped over the ridge and then down the upper part of the party wall. Cedar boarding is also used on the gable, with some elements of the timber frame exposed. This relatively unorthodox solution also involves wood-fibre insulation and wood-fibre sarking, using products from

Western Red Cedar timber-boarded roof and walls in Hackney, London; the boarding is placed over insulating sarking boards made of water-resistant wood fibre, designed by Flacq Architects.

Natural Building Technologies, creating a breathable roof without a plastic membrane. The cedar boards have been imported and are fixed with stainless steel pins to closely spaced battens.

Tiles and Slates

There is a wide range of natural slates available for roofing. Slate quarried in North Wales and the Lake District were the main sources of supply. Today, British-quarried slate is very expensive and most slate products are imported from Spain, China and other parts of the world. Ethical concerns about the standards imposed in distant quarries and the energy costs of transport may put off many natural builders.

Recycled slates are still available but are also expensive. However, slates do enhance the natural look of a building. But despite this, buildings are still being demolished without the slates being removed for recycling.

Natural clay tiles are as attractive as slates but require firing like bricks, thus using a lot of energy and contributing to carbon emissions. Nevertheless, in many parts of the country planning policies require the use of traditional-looking roof coverings. Synthetic, fibre-cement 'slates' and concrete tiles have an artificial look, which is uncomfortable on natural buildings. 'Slates' made from recycled rubber are also now available.

Recycled slates, when available, are still the best option for roofing; the 'Solar-Twin' panel has been retrofitted but some solar panels are now coming on to the market that can be integrated into a new roof.

PLANTED ROOFS

For many people, green or planted roofs are synonymous with natural or ecological buildings. In the early days of ecological architecture in Germany in particular, almost every innovative building had a green roof. One of the seminal green buildings in Britain is the Nant-y-Cwm kindergarten in Pembrokeshire in Wales. Designed and built by the architect Christopher Day and many volunteers (including the author), this tiny building has influenced many in their thinking about ecological building. In fact, many of the materials used, including those for the roof, would not be regarded as environmentally friendly today, but the building cost little

and used whatever materials could be found and donated. The simple design of the grass roof, using old carpet and polypropylene netting, became a working detail in the *Architects' Journal* and established the idea of planted roofs made from components rather than expensive proprietary systems.

The idea of planted roofs spread in Germany because it was possible to negotiate a discount on local taxes by reducing the water run-off from buildings. Most planted roofs will absorb and then discharge 30 to 50 per cent of rainwater through evaporation. Planted roofs were also common in Scandinavia on traditional buildings, where pitch-coated timbers were then covered with sods. Many

The green roof at the Nant-y-Cwm kindergarten in Pembrokeshire, built by the architect Christopher Day and many volunteers.

slightly moist. On the other hand, a planted roof will help to reduce the solar gain to a roof, reducing the expansion and contraction of the roofing materials and preventing the building from overheating if the insulation is inadequate. There is stronger evidence that a green roof will reduce the cooling load.

The second myth is that a planted roof will create significant biodiversity on top of your building. Quite absurd claims are made in some of the advertising literature about the sort of wildlife that will inhabit planted roofs. In reality, most planted roofs will have no more impact on biodiversity than the average lawn and will attract only limited wildlife. In some cases the wildlife will be unwelcome and will destroy the planting, but the wilder the roof the greater the biodiversity. Yet the concept of replacing the ground that has been destroyed under a building with a green area on top has to be of significant environmental benefit, particularly in cities. The plants convert carbon dioxide to oxygen and cool the surfaces, which can radiate heat in cities.

The third myth is that it is necessary to mow a grass roof and water it when the weather is hot and dry. If it is a requirement that the planted roof should look like a golf course or a bowling green, then it will be necessary to water and mow, but it is not advisable to put machinery on to such a roof, as the waterproof membrane and the planting could be damaged. One of the most beautiful aspects of a grass roof is the way it changes colours with the seasons, from a lush green to a wispy hay colour. Even when the grass appears to have died it will all come to life again.

The use of succulent plants has become common with planted roofs since there is no need for a thick layer of soil. Occasionally it is possible to see a goat tethered on a grass roof, but this is because there is good grass for the goat and not as a form of maintenance. Some companies and consultants advocate

rural cottages in Ireland were also covered in sod roofs, but this did not guarantee a waterproof building. Today, planted roofs provide an attractive option for natural builders seeking a reasonably economical and durable roofing solution that will be in harmony with other natural and ecological materials and finishes.

There are a number of myths about planted roofs. First, it is assumed that they provide additional thermal insulation to a roof, thus reducing heat loss. This is not necessarily the case, and a saturated planted roof may have the opposite effect. However, some companies claim that there can be a 25 per cent increase in insulation when the roof is dry or only

OPPOSITE: Thrift Cottage in Hertfordshire, built by Lydia and Robert Somerville, is a timber-frame building, timber-clad and with a grass roof and intended to be a model for sustainable living; it has a very high level of cellulose and wool insulation, a dry compost toilet and many other ecological features.

A planted roof with a variety of plants and flowers that can survive on little growing medium.

irrigation systems for green roofs, but as water becomes in shorter supply in some parts of the United Kingdom, to use mains water for this may be illegal. It would therefore be necessary to install rain-water-harvesting systems to provide the water to irrigate the roof. This is a slightly contradictory concept because planted roofs will still collect their own rainwater. However, in semi-arid areas, such as the southeast of England, some water storage and irrigation may be necessary.

The fourth myth is the need to spend a lot of money on thick root barriers to prevent roots from penetrating the structure below the waterproof or structural layers. In reality, the potential for plants or trees to cause serious root damage is largely governed by the thickness of soil or the planting medium on the roof. In my experience, a wide range of green grasses and plants will thrive on a relatively thin layer of soil, 50mm or even less. Trees and other deep-rooting plants will rarely become established in such conditions. Also, if the grass is allowed to die off and then regrow, other plants will not survive. Root barriers are necessary where there is a thicker layer of soil. Many of the proprietary green-roofing systems advocate significant depths of substrate and water-retention layers, as well as the growing medium, with depths of up to 150mm to allow roots to become established. The thicker the layer of growing

Unwelcome 'biodiversity' on a planted roof: the sedum roof at the highly energy-efficient Heeley City Farm building in Sheffield, where pigeons have destroyed much of it; no doubt attracted by the animal feed around the farm, it would be hard to keep them away.

medium, the heavier the roof will become and the greater the cost as the structure has to be significantly strengthened.

The main reasons for choosing a planted roof, in order of importance, are:

1. that they provide an economical and low-maintenance solution to what to put on the roof;
2. because of their attractive appearance which can enhance the natural appearance of a building;
3. that it is a way of creating an environmentally friendly surface.

The second reason is not an easy option for many architects, however, particularly when there is a fashion for minimalist or modernist buildings. Many

architects hate the idea of what they call 'hairy' buildings and thus they go to great lengths either to hide the planted part of the roof or to design a roof edge detail which means that unkempt grass does not hang down over the clean lines of their building. Of course, it is important to detail the edge of a grass roof so that gutters and down spouts do not become blocked with vegetation, but experience shows that planted roofs behave themselves remarkably well and require very little maintenance. If the decision is made to have a natural roof then it seems only logical to let it look natural and not try to treat planting as some synthetic product.

Due to the growing popularity of planted roofs, a number of roofing companies have introduced planted roof systems that include the whole roof

A grass roof can be a useful way to hide a building or part of the earth sheltering a building; the grass will grow long, then turn yellow, die back and then grow again.

Lean-to roof being re-laid with an EPDM membrane over plywood decking.

build-up and the green material on top. These are generally specified because they come with a warranty and architects feel that this minimizes their risk. On the other hand, such roof systems are very expensive and in most cases far from being natural or green. This is because the waterproofing and insulation systems which are employed use synthetic, fossil-fuel-based products.

The companies that charge highly for proprietary green-roof systems are arguing strongly for codes of practice, which will ensure that builders and architects will be required to use complicated warranted systems. These companies are working with organizations such as the Construction Industry Research

OPPOSITE: A sedum roof made up from separately supplied elements: a timber-boarded roof, EPDM membrane and then covered with a sedum mat; architect: Rachel Bevan.

and Information Association (CIRIA) towards such guidance, according to Austin Williams (*Architects' Journal*, 7 July 2005). There is a danger that, should codes of practice become rigid standards, this may make it more difficult to get approval for self-designed planted roofs. This is justified because of the idea that clients will want long-term guarantees. This is partly because of bad experience with leaking flat roofs in the past, but not everyone in the industry has the same view. At a conference on green roofs, the secretary of the Single Ply Roofing Association said, 'There will undoubtedly be a drive to manufacture and provide "systems" as opposed to components in the future' (Hooker, *Architects' Journal*, ibid.). Hooker questioned the concept of warranties, suggesting instead that, 'A client would be reasonable in asking for a guarantee covering the initial setting up period, but not effectively into perpetuity.' Thus, when deciding what sort of green or living roof to install, there is a choice between buying a complete

The grass mat is put back, complete with second-hand carpet and polypropylene netting.

Within three to four weeks, with only a little rain in August, the grass is green again.

system and making up your own design using good quality components.

Planted roof systems involve a waterproof membrane, insulation layers, some of which are designed with pockets to hold the growing medium, root membranes, filter fleeces and a range of substrates and growing media. Some companies offer mats that are impregnated with plants and can simply be rolled out to give an 'instant' green roof. Others use what is known as 'hydro-planting' and can spray a slurry of growing medium and seeds on to the roof.

The main concern about proprietary systems, from an environmental point of view, is the waterproofing and roof build-up materials that are used. These include aluminium, steel and PVC. Interestingly, the composition of the waterproof membranes is rarely described in manufacturer's literature and the natural builder will have to interrogate suppliers for details. In many cases the materials used involve a range of plastic products that are harmful to the environment. It seems somewhat illogical to use such materials for a planted roof, which is meant to be 'green'. PVC is the least attractive material for the natural builder because of the wide range of environmental negatives of this material, including dioxin waste, which is one of the most toxic pollutants in the ecosystem, heavy metals and other additives, and the difficulty in disposing of or recycling PVC. Due to the many criticisms of the material and moves to ban it completely, the plastics industry has made some moves to reduce the hazards associated with it, but, applying the precautionary principle, it would seem advisable to avoid green roof systems which use PVC (which at present means most of them).

The Green Building Handbook recommends EPDM (ethylene propylene diene monomer, a synthetic rubber, commonly known as butyl and often used for pond liners) as the least environmentally damaging, synthetic, waterproof membrane, although it is still a fossil-fuel-based product. It is claimed to be the most durable of polymeric membranes and able to cope with temperature changes better than other materials. Blends of polypropylene and EPDM are now available commonly referred to as TPO. EPDM is normally black but TPO is available in a range of colours, but this is rarely of any relevance for a planted roof. It is possible to create planted roofs with an EPDM or TPO membrane for waterproofing by using simple materials that are inexpensive which, if done with care, will last as long as a warranted system. It is important that the roof structure and decking are strong enough to take the weight of a planted roof; much of the weight is in the absorbed water or snow loadings. It is always important here to take the advice of a structural engineer, even for a small building.

The waterproof membrane is then laid on the roof and soil or turfs spread or laid on top. In most places in the United Kingdom and Ireland it is not necessary to seed the roof as the roof will self-seed. Self-seeding will reflect the natural local biodiversity much better than a sprayed-on slurry and will change over the year and over time. Normally 50–75 mm of mixed soil and light gravel will be sufficient. Flat roofs should have a slight gradient to encourage drainage. For pitched roofs it is necessary to be a little more ingenious. We have used second-hand carpet laid on top of the waterproof membrane and then a layer of polypropylene bean netting, which is stretched over the roof and secured so that it does not slip. Once the grass and roots become established, they knit into the netting and carpet and a solid planted mat remains. If the roof pitch is steep it is important to provide an edge detail to prevent the material from slipping down the roof. Some architects have attempted very steep planted roofs, but these are not to be recommended.

It is best to create a 'warm roof' in which the insulation is placed on top of the waterproof membrane. It is difficult to use a natural insulating product and one of the synthetic insulation products is the most usual. On a pitched roof it is important to secure the insulation with polypropylene netting, and this is not easy on a breezy day.

In order to demonstrate the simplicity of self-designed, planted roofs the accompanying series of photographs shows a sloping, planted roof which was removed because the original membrane had been some left-over, cheap, damp-proof plastic and roofing felt. The grass mat was peeled off and the waterproof layer was replaced with an EPDM sheet. The grass mat was simply put back on. Even though it looks dead during a dry August, with rain it is green again within four weeks (*see* pages 111–112).

CHAPTER 6

Lime and Masonry

LIME

Natural building has had a significant impact on the use of lime in building. Lime has been in use for building for thousands of years and was widely used where limestone is available. Old maps of places such as Donegal show a limekiln in almost every field by the roadside. However, lime was gradually replaced when Portland cement was invented, which is also made from limestone but fired in a rotary kiln. When mixed with sand and stone, modern concrete could be made. Cement seemed to have advantages, it was cheap, easier to use and dried more quickly. Since then the cement and concrete industry has dominated the construction industry.

Traditional lime was revived when it was realized that it was necessary to restore old buildings, and gradually the advantages of lime over cement were recognized. Lime is soft, permeable, and elastic and has a high capillarity. Cement, on the other hand, is hard, impermeable and inflexible, and has a low capillarity. This means that lime-based and cement-based materials can perform quite differently. Considerable damage has been done to great monuments and simple vernacular cottages by the ignorant use of cement instead of lime. The United Kingdom Building Limes Forum has done an enormous amount of work to raise an awareness of lime and to develop expertise. As a result, it is now possible to buy good quality building limes, of several types, throughout the United Kingdom and Ireland. There are specialists available to give advice and training and lime may be used in conjunction with other natural materials such as hemp.

Lime can be shown to be more sustainable, environmentally-friendly and better with naturally breathing buildings than cement, although there are also situations in which cement and concrete may be more appropriate. Lime takes less energy to produce, with much lower carbon emissions, because it uses kilns at a lower temperature. Lime has advantages in being softer, more flexible and more appropriate for natural materials. Sometimes it is assumed that lime is good and cement is bad, but this is not a helpful dichotomy; cement is really just another form of lime and may be better in some circumstances. Furthermore, cement companies are now producing lime, but many natural builders will prefer to source theirs from a specialist local lime producer who also supplies other natural materials.

Lime is produced by heating calcium carbonate (limestone, chalk, shells, coral, for example) in a kiln to a temperature of about 900°C. At this temperature carbon dioxide is given off and the calcium carbonate is chemically changed to form calcium oxide (here known as quicklime). Lime may be used in several forms, but all originate from quicklime. Water and quicklime are combined in a process known as hydration to produce hydrated lime. The normal product is a dry powder, sold in bags and generally known as hydrated lime or lime hydrate. If more water is added the process is normally referred to as 'slaking', which creates the lime putty usually sold in plastic tubs.

The properties of the dry hydrate or putty will depend mainly on the source of calcium carbonate burned and, in particular, the impurities it contained. Very pure sources of calcium carbonate, such as Buxton limestone, will produce pure quicklime and

Bags of hydraulic lime at Mike Wye Building Supplies in Devon; lime comes in different strengths, these bags from Castle Cement are NHL5, which is high strength; feebler lime is labelled 2.5 and 3.5.

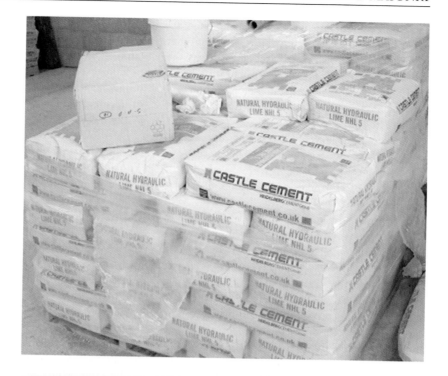

Most parts of England, Wales and Ireland now have local specialist suppliers of good quality lime such as Ty Mawr, who can also supply other materials and advise on the best materials to use.

hence pure putties. Pure lime putty (calcium hydroxide) is known as 'fat lime'; it will not set under water and is therefore stored with a layer of water over the top. Hydrated lime and lime putty can be mixed with sand and aggregates, normally in the proportion of 1 part of lime to 3 of sand, and turned into mortars and plasters.

Lime mortar remains soft and flexible and is therefore much better for brickwork. Cement mortars can be too strong, which encourages the weathering of softer bricks. Blocks and bricks laid with lime mortar can easily be recycled, whereas brick walls with cement mortars can only be broken up and used as fill. When lime is used in building, water is lost during the initial setting and the material continues to absorb carbon dioxide, gradually returning to calcium carbonate, but this is quite a slow process.

Limestones that contain clay or silicates produce building limes that are known as 'hydraulic' because they have the ability to set under water. The impurities, sometimes referred to as pozzolans, contain silica, alumina and iron compounds that give the limes a more complicated chemistry. The particular properties of hydraulic limes are due to the amount of impurity in the burned limestone: the greater the impurity, the faster the set and the harder the mortar. In Roman times volcanic dust from Pozzouli, near Naples (hence the name pozzolan), was added to lime so that it became artificially hydraulic. Crushed bricks or tiles were also used to similar effect.

Lime is relatively weak in both compression and tension and this gives masonry walls constructed with lime mortar a certain amount of flexibility. Each mortar joint, although well bonded to the masonry, has the ability to act as a tiny expansion joint. Where cracks do appear they are normally invisible (micro-cracking). In this way it is possible for walls constructed with lime mortar to expand, contract and flex, healing themselves as micro-cracking occurs. Cement, by contrast, is quite strong in tension and will try to resist movement. The tensile forces within a wall build up, transmitted by the cement mortar from one masonry unit to the next until they become too great to withstand. At this point, if there is no expansion joint, a crack will form. The crack is likely to be quite major and will run right through the

masonry and the mortar joints, finding the line of least resistance. This type of crack does not have the ability to heal itself and may become a structural defect (certainly a point for water ingress). The same property can be observed in cement-based renders, where cracking is quite typical and troublesome. Portland cement may be an ideal material for structural concrete but it is no longer a good one for mortars, plasters and renders in a sustainable construction industry. Lime and cement are similar in their production methods and raw materials, but ordinary Portland cement is used inappropriately in many buildings.

I have observed that it is a mistake to see the differences between cement and lime as 'cement bad, lime good'. Many cement companies are realizing that there is a market for lime and are changing their production. Much good quality lime is currently imported from France, where traditional lime renders and mortars have survived more successfully, but both the United Kingdom and Ireland have good quality limestone and lime production may increase. Portland cement will still be used in civil engineering and major structures; however, even with cement there are alternatives that have environmental benefits, such as using fly ash. Not only can fly ash concrete provide a solution for dealing with power-station waste, but it can also produce better and stronger concretes, as explained in a book by Bruce King, of the Ecological Building Network.

Hydrated or 'air limes' and the weaker hydraulic limes are most suitable for the conservation and repair of historic buildings. They are ideal for most normal low-rise, domestic/commercial buildings, which is good news for natural builders since the increasing availability of lime will bring down costs. It is now possible to obtain pre-mixed, dry mortars in storage silos and high-shear mixers. This simply requires a connection to electricity and water to

OPPOSITE: The Lhoist quarry near Buxton, Derbyshire produces some of the purest lime in Europe with some of the most efficient kilns; however, quarrying and lime burning have environmental impacts, if not as great as those of cement manufacture.

enable it to produce quality-controlled lime mortar at the touch of a button. Lime mortar is also useful in conjunction with timber; the ability to draw moisture away from timber and allow it to evaporate safely is essential in keeping timber in good condition, added to which lime is a natural biocide and can then help to protect timber from decay and insect attack.

The main advantages of lime are summarized below (the author thanks Ian Pritchett of Limetec for this summary):

- the use of lime-based mortars can avoid having to use expansion/movement joints
- lime is flexible
- lime-based materials have a lower embodied energy; a typical lime-based mortar will have 50 to 70 per cent of the embodied energy of an equivalent cement-based mortar; in addition, they re-absorb some of the carbon dioxide on carbonation that was emitted during their manufacture
- the use of lime allows masonry (bricks and stones) to be recycled; cement-based mortars can turn brick into an unsustainable material
- lime enables low-energy, sustainable materials to be used; materials such as reeds, straw, timber, hemp and clay can be used as construction materials
- moisture can easily evaporate from the surface of lime-based materials
- lime-based materials can create healthier living environments; this is because they are hygroscopic and permeable, allowing for the transfer of moisture from the internal to the external environment
- there is less waste when using lime-based materials; hydraulic lime can be typically reworked for up to 24hr after it has been mixed with water
- lime is visually more attractive and can bring out the beauty of masonry
- lime mortars have a proven durability
- lime can be supplied in the form of pre-mixed, dry mortars.

Spray applications of lime plasters are also an advantage, with hydraulic limes producing much better plasters and renders than cement and which can be applied at a rate up to four times faster than a man with a hawk and trowel.

Demonstrations and training in the use of lime are available at a number of centres, including Limetec in Henley.

Lime renders with mineral paints can provide a more flexible and attractive render that is better for use with timber-frame buildings, such as in this lower-cost dwelling at the Wintles Eco Village in Shropshire.

Traditional lime putty and sand should be used for stone pointing; the capping to the wall is made with hydraulic lime as it is more durable.

Stone without mortar has been used by Andy Clayden, a landscape architect in Sheffield, for a small garden room; even in small quantities stone can enhance the feeling of buildings. (Photo: Andy Clayden)

Up until the eighteenth century most buildings in the United Kingdom were rendered. In parts of the country where the weather is more severe this tradition has continued, but in areas with more moderate weather, facing brick has become more fashionable. Most countries in Europe still have a tradition for render and this is an important factor contributing to the longevity of their buildings. In this country render is likely to be used more frequently in the future because of the effects of climate change. Insulating renders are being used to retrofit existing buildings, although this is usually with a lime-base material with added polymers. Polymer-insulated renders are not as environmentally friendly as those made of natural materials and lime, because they do not provide breathable finishes. However, polymer science will converge with the development of natural fibres and products and polymer products will become available based on natural oils and crop-based materials.

STONE AND OTHER MASONRY

Dressed stone has always been a luxury material and largely reserved for prestige and public buildings. Stone cladding as a natural material is still widely used on buildings, but purely as a skin over concrete,

A stone porch, made from material found on site, for a building which is otherwise built of straw bale and timber, reinforces the importance of security about the entrance.

with the need for stainless steel bolts and hangers. However, natural stone, discarded in quarries or simply dug out of the ground on site, can be used for natural building in a number of ways.

Traditional vernacular houses and barns were built from fieldstones by the use of a number of rubble walling methods. Rubble stonewalls are not suitable today for structural walls and will not provide adequate air-tightness or insulation or be sufficiently weatherproof, but stone facing may be an option if the stone is available. Recycled stone can usually be obtained, although at a price. Sadly, the demand for stone for imposing gateways leads to the unnecessary demolition of old buildings. Stone facing and walling

should be built with an appropriate lime mortar and not cement; this allows the wall to flex and the stones can be recycled in the future. Stones or slate can be used for windowsills with careful detailing. Small rubble stonewalls may also be essential as the base for cob or straw-bale walls.

Drystone walling is a traditional technique, with many methods and styles, in areas where there was plenty of stone. A wall constructed in this way may be useful as a rain screen where other materials behind are able to deal with some driving rain getting through. Gabions are also becoming fashionable in which techniques, initially developed for civil engineering such as riverbank construction, have become

A stone plinth is traditional for cob walls, although, in this Kevin McCabe house, the foundations and the plinth are also well insulated.

an architectural motif. Instead of using crude quarry stone to fill gabions, more attractive, leftover stone can be used. Again this can be used as a rain screen or simply for garden retaining walls.

CORDWOOD AND LIME

This is a form of building with short lengths of round-wood timber logs. It is usually referred to as masonry, which is why it is in this chapter. Normally the logs are set in a lime mortar with an insulation gap in the middle. It is seen as a cheap way to build since it can use up scrap wood and it is claimed to give a good standard of insulation. Cordwood can look attractive, but it is hard to believe that it is particularly durable or provides a good standard of insulation. The log ends will be vulnerable to water penetration and splitting and they provide a cold bridge through the wall, together with the mortar which normally represents about 40 per cent of the wall in which they are embedded. However, it is a popular technique with some natural builders.

A gabion wall, using quarry stone, in a typical civil engineering setting, but increasingly used as a rain screen or decorative feature in building design.

Cordwood used in Caroline Barry's house in Somerset.

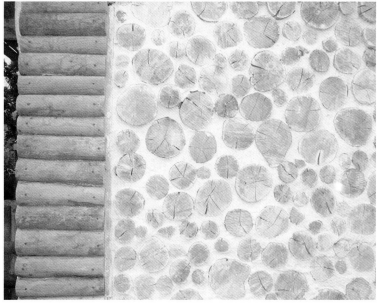

Hemp

It is thought that hemp was used in buildings as early as Roman times. The value of a hemp and lime mix was first discovered as an ideal replacement for wattle and daub in historic timber-frame structures.

Hemp is used in a wide range of construction materials and is also referred to in Chapter 8. In this chapter the use of hemp composites to create walls and floors of buildings is discussed. While hemp construction has been common in France for over a decade, it is a relatively new idea in the United Kingdom. Thus, while there were only a few examples to illustrate this chapter, hemp construction is likely to become more commonplace over the next few years.

THE DEVELOPMENT OF HEMP CONSTRUCTION

There are now several hundred hemp houses in France; non-domestic buildings have also used hemp and a large building is currently on site in Clermont Ferrand for the French Environment Ministry, which will be using hemp and lime block infill for the walls. Approximately 4,000 tonnes of hemp shive are used annually for building in France, representing an industry worth over £20 million. While this is still very small in terms of mainstream construction, hemp-composite technology has attracted the interest of the aerated concrete block manufacturers and the main hemp and lime materials suppliers in France are now part of the Lhoist group, the biggest manufacturer of industrial lime in the world.

Several houses incorporating hemp have been built in the south-east of England, including a housing association scheme in Haverhill, Essex, for the Suffolk Housing Society. This project, pioneered by Ralph Carpenter of Modece Architects, used a hemp building system developed by the French company Isochanvre. Isochanvre is no longer in business but the Haverhill scheme was monitored and evaluated by the BRE and their reports are easily downloaded from websites. The Haverhill project has been successful, with satisfaction recorded by both tenants and the housing association. Carpenter has continued to work with hemp building in other projects.

Because the use of hemp in construction is relatively new in the UK and Ireland, there are no official guidelines or British Standards yet. Those who have used hemp are pioneers and have taken a risk that the material would work as was hoped. However, a number of businesses and professionals have come together to form a trade association to promote and develop the use of hemp in construction and will in time develop technical guidance and advice.

THE GROWING AND PROCESSING OF HEMP

Before discussing how to construct buildings with hemp, it is worth looking at how it is grown and made available as a building material. Hemp and flax were commonly grown throughout Europe, but hemp became illegal in many countries, particularly the USA, because of its association with the drug marijuana. Industrial hemp, grown from seed varieties that are low in THC (tetrahydrocannabinol) and thus drug-free, can look similar to marijuana in the field, but it has no psychotropic properties.

Handmade tiles by County Down schoolchildren in a hemp wall at the Chelsea Flower Show, 2004; designer: Celia Spouncer. (Photo: Celia Spouncer)

Demonstration of hemp and lime infill to an historic timber frame in Troyes, France.

Ralph Carpenter's house in Suffolk, built with hemp lime walls and floors.

Hemp growing on a farm in Northern Ireland; several varieties have been successfully grown, suitable for fibre and also for seed, without pesticide or fertilizer.

Hemp was essential for sail cloth and rope-making and was central to the naval prowess of Britain; however, nylon gradually replaced natural fibre and the synthetic fibre industries have played their part in getting hemp banned, a subject popular with conspiracy theorists!

Today, it is possible to grow hemp with government and police permission and licences are relatively easy to obtain. Agricultural subsidies were available for hemp growing at one time but have now been limited, and thus it is not so attractive as a crop to the farmer without a market for it. In the United Kingdom Hemcore is the main company processing hemp, and farmers throughout the south of England supply hemp bales to its factory in Essex. There are also a number of smaller companies trying to process hemp. It will become more readily available as more processing plants are opened so that the farmer does not need to transport it for great distances.

Hemp Street in East Belfast shows how historically significant hemp was to the British and Irish economy.

OPPOSITE: *Suffolk Housing Society hemp houses in Haverhill; two simple, modest, low-cost houses that may have a fundamental effect on the future of the building industry in Britain and Ireland; the adjacent brick-faced houses were built to be identical so that their performance could be compared with that of the hemp houses.*

A car interior made from a hemp/resin composite, one example of the many bio- and eco-composites that are being developed.

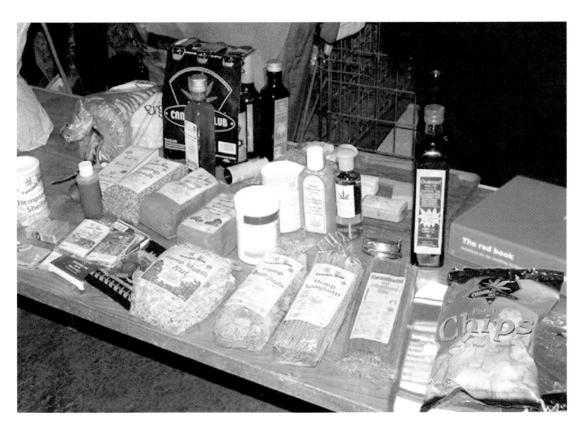

The processing involves major investment, since specialized equipment needs to be used. The decortication of the hemp is sometimes carried out by using a hammer mill but this damages the fibre. Hemp needs to be 'retted' so that the fibre can be more easily broken down and there are several ways in which this can be done. The plant stalks are usually fed into a machine that strips off the fibre that is then used for a number of natural fibre composites, ranging from clothing to car interiors. The owners of top-of-the-range German cars may be surprised to hear that their car is made from hemp. The remaining stalks of the plant are chopped up, dried, dust is removed and the stalks are sold in bales for horse bedding. The horse bedding is attractive as it absorbs a lot of water and does not need to be changed as often as ordinary straw or sawdust. Some people also think that it is therapeutic for the horses.

Hemp can also be grown for seed, which is rich in oils and can be used in cosmetics and foodstuffs ranging from hemp ice cream to shampoos and massage oils. For many, hemp is a wonder crop and it is hard for supporters to understand why it is not grown more widely. Ironically, for an environmentally beneficial crop, it has been kept alive through its use in high-quality cigarette papers. Hemp is much better for paper manufacture than wood, with no chemical by-products and a high cellulose content. Unfortunately, its association with the drug varieties has undoubtedly made its cultivation controversial and held back research and the development of hemp products and applications.

The woody core of the plant, known as the 'hurd' or 'shive', is chopped up, cleaned of dust and sold as horse bedding; this material is also being used for building.

THE BASICS OF HEMP CONSTRUCTION

To use hemp as a building material involves mixing it with some other material such as lime or earth. This is referred to here as 'hempcrete'. Hempcrete can be used as a solid wall, much like concrete, either free-standing, combined with timber frame or as an infill within a post and beam structure. It can also be cast as blocks and used as an insulating plaster.

The 'conventional' method of hemp construction involves casting hempcrete around some form of timber frame. The frame may be constructed on site or in prefabricated panels and could be supplied by any normal timber-frame company. The frame that is designed to carry the structural loads creates the structural integrity of the building and the hempcrete is used simply as a form of solid wall insulation around the timber frame.

OPPOSITE: A huge variety of products can be made from hemp, including breakfast cereal, beer, shampoo, chips, spaghetti and oils; it is a versatile material, held back in its development because of prejudice about its relationship with marijuana.

A timber frame constructed and ready for hemp to be cast; project by The Old Builders Company. (Photo: Henry Thompson)

An internal wall in the Suffolk Housing Society hemp houses in Haverhill; this shows the shuttering partially removed, the plywood sheets were taken off immediately the hemp was placed; hemp and lime were used for the internal walls due to the mixture's good acoustic properties.

Different kinds of timber frames can be used; normal timber-frame construction involves a complex, built up frame, sheathing boards, vapour barriers and insulation quilts or sometimes blown-in cellulose. However, by using hempcrete, cast around the timber frame, both the racking resistance and insulation are provided in one step. The result is a solid breathing wall that requires a render or other external cladding to protect it from the weather. The thickness of the wall can range from 200 to 500mm. There should be at least 50mm of cover on the timber frame externally. If the shuttering is removed carefully, the exposed hemp lime wall does not need to be plastered internally. Thus the attraction of using solid hempcrete walls is that it simplifies and reduces the number of layers and processes involved in timber-frame construction. But solid wall construction is still viewed with some scepticism by insurers in the United Kingdom and it may take some time to persuade regulatory bodies, valuation surveyors, insurance and warranty schemes that this form of construction is acceptable.

Mixing Hempcrete

Hempcrete is made by mixing chopped up hemp, which comes from the shive or hurd of the plant, and then mixing it with either lime or earth. The mixture can be made by hand, or in a normal cement mixer. A horizontal paddle mixer, adapted for hemp mixing, is better, however, as the mix tends to ball in a cement mixer. Water is added to the dry mix, and it is important not to add too much. Once the material is properly mixed together and all the lime powder has been absorbed, the mix can be placed by shovel or some other means into timber shuttering. It looks a little like wet, recycled cellulose for those who are familiar with this material. The mix is tamped into the shuttering to ensure that it is properly packed in. As soon as it is in place, the shuttering can be removed. It is not necessary to oil the shuttering, but, if it is left in place too long, the mix will stick to it and it will be almost impossible to remove. The shuttering is packed out using timber or plastic spacers around long screws that are screwed to the time frame. Packing out the shuttering is necessary to provide 50mm or more cover of the hempcrete around the timer frame.

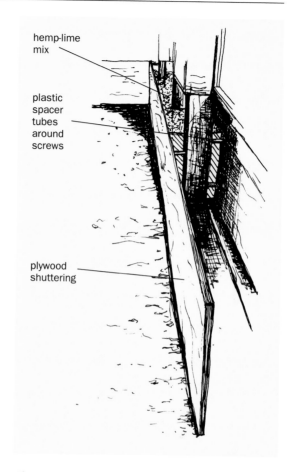

hemp-lime mix

plastic spacer tubes around screws

plywood shuttering

Shuttering around a timber frame; note the plastic spacer tubes to give the timber frame at least 50mm cover – these can be removed since the long screws are extracted with the shuttering.

Spraying Hempcrete

In France, some houses are constructed of timber frame by using an internal, permanent shuttering with plasterboard or fibreboard; this forms the internal finish. The hemp-lime mix is then sprayed into the walls by using specialist equipment. When the mix is applied, a dry mixture of hemp and lime is pumped down a large pipe by a powerful compressor and water is added in the right quantity at the nozzle. The spraying is quick and efficient and makes the use of hemp and lime cost-effective when compared with other forms of wall construction and insulation.

Placing the hempcrete mix into the shuttering. (Photo: Henry Thompson)

Mixing the hempcrete in a conventional cement mixer. (Photo: Henry Thompson)

However, the investment required to buy the equipment is substantial and it will require a greater uptake of this method before it becomes commonplace.

Making hempcrete with hemp and lime is a simple process and can be learned by any joiner, contractor or DIY builder very quickly. However, there are some things that can go wrong and it is important to ensure that the correct materials and mixture are used and that there is rigorous quality control during the construction process. There is already some evidence that self-build enthusiasts have found out about hemp building through the Internet and have, as a result, constructed sub-standard buildings because they have not had proper professional advice.

TREATED OR MINERALIZED HEMP AND POSSIBLE PROBLEMS

Buildings have been constructed using hemp shives mixed with lime, which are normally sold for horse bedding. One French company was marketing 'mineralized' hemp in which the hemp hurds had been treated in some way. This treatment was secret and several suggestions have been made as to the additives. It was claimed that the mineralized hemp was longer lasting and that untreated hemp would rot or grown mould or mushrooms. Some experiments have been made with inconclusive results and little apparent difference between 'mineralized' and untreated hemp. As with all natural materials discussed in this book, great care has to be taken to protect the material and ensure that it is kept dry and mixed correctly. Any natural material can rot and decay if not handled or used properly. The lime should provide some protection from rot and insect attack because lime is highly alkaline and a natural biocide. However, more research needs to be done before firm conclusions can be drawn about the durability of hempcrete.

A small paddle mixer especially adapted to mix hempcrete.

Hemp and lime being sprayed into a timber frame; the water comes in a separate pipe and is mixed at the nozzle. (Photo: Henry Thompson)

The compressor used to pump the hemp mix for spraying. (Photo: Henry Thompson)

Large paddle mixer for the hemp and lime before the mixture is pumped. (Photo: Henry Thompson)

A test section of hempcrete wall made with horse-bedding hemp and hydraulic lime, 300mm thick, left exposed to Ulster rain and weather for two years; even though this has not been rendered and despite being a little green on top there are few signs of deterioration.

Scientific research carried out in France has suggested that the role of water in a hemp mix is crucial because hemp will absorb a substantial amount of it. This research has shown that the other material that is mixed with hemp, such as lime, can be starved of water and thus the mix will not gain its full strength if the lime fails to carbonate properly. In some tests, hemp blocks have been sawn open and it was discovered that some of the lime in the centre was still in powder form and had not properly mixed and carbonated. Thus some French companies argue that it is important to use a lime binder that can cope with the competition between the hemp and lime for the water. They have developed special mixes of lime to deal with this potential problem. One of these is known as Tradical 70, which is a mixture of air-lime (hydrated lime), some natural hydraulic lime, a pozzolan and a small biological additive. But companies experimenting with hemp in the United Kingdom have successfully used hydraulic limes and other mixes. St Astier Lime have developed a lime binder called 'Batichanvre' to use with hemp.

Another possible problem is that if too much water is used the walls can take a long time to dry out. Lime is much slower to dry than cement, and anyone building with hemp and lime must not expect hempcrete to behave like concrete. It also takes much longer to gain its full strength. For this reason it is most important that anyone embarking on hemp construction should use the correct materials and seek specialist advice from architects and suppliers who are familiar with them.

The ability of hemp to absorb moisture is also a useful feature of the material because, in consequence, it can help to moderate humidity in a building. As long as a hemp wall can breathe and water vapour can pass through it, then the wall can dry out again. This makes the material potentially attractive as a plaster for masonry walls. Accelerated weathering tests at the Building Research Establishment and experience in France suggest that the composite material has good durability and the ability, if properly rendered, to withstand weathering. However, it is important not to case hempcrete or use lime renders during very cold or frosty weather.

PROPORTIONS OF MATERIALS IN HEMPCRETE

It is not easy to give detailed instructions on the correct proportions of hemp and lime as scientific work is still in progress to determine this. The manufacturers of specialist hemp-lime binders provide details which vary depending on whether other materials such as sand are to be added. Approximately 1 part of lime to 3 or 4 of hemp is used. The new Hemp Lime

A corner of a hempcrete wall shortly after casting. (Photo: Henry Thompson)

Construction Products Association will be producing technical guidance notes.

STRUCTURAL STRENGTH

The hempcrete takes about two to three weeks to dry out, depending on local conditions, as it is slower to dry than conventional concrete. The lime continues to gain in strength over the subsequent few years as it naturally carbonates. However, once the shuttering is removed the wall is stable. It should be protected from rain with sheeting and possible vandal damage should be avoided because the walls are initially quite soft.

The hempcrete has reasonably good structural strength, sufficient for low-rise, load-bearing and non-load-bearing panels. It has cube strength in the region of 0.2 to $1.0N/mm^2$, but in compression tests at Queen's University, Belfast, where test blocks included hemp fibre, they were just within the British Standard range for concrete blocks. The composite is quite flexible and shrinkage cracks are unusual. The hempcrete can provide racking resistance to the timber frame, obviating the need for bracing or sheathing boards. When hempcrete is cast around timber frame it is not load-bearing. There should be little difficulty from a structural point of view using hempcrete for small, domestic-size buildings, provided that a timber frame is used for the structure.

More recently, as experiments have continued on different proportions of hemp and lime, it has been discovered that it is possible to create strong composites, which can perform similarly to concrete. However, the stronger the mix, the heavier and denser the material, with more lime and less hemp, giving a lower insulation value. The density and the strength appear to be in inverse proportion to the level of insulation. Further research will help to determine the best proportions of hemp and binders for different requirements.

HEMP BLOCKS

Instead of casting hempcrete as a composite around a timber frame, blocks can be produced. Blocks can be manufactured in a factory and are therefore not subject to weather conditions. They can then be laid as an infill to a frame construction. The blocks will need a lime mortar and may have to be laid on their side to gain adequate strength and insulation. Currently, this is a more expensive option and loses many of the benefits of cast hempcrete.

Aukett Fitzroy Robinson Architects and Lister Beare Engineers have designed a major hemp construction for a distribution warehouse for Adnams' Brewery in Suffolk. In this case hemp blocks are to be used as infill between and around a conventional, portal steel frame. The wall is to be 500mm thick and it was decided to have two walls of block with a hempcrete in-situ mix cast around the columns and

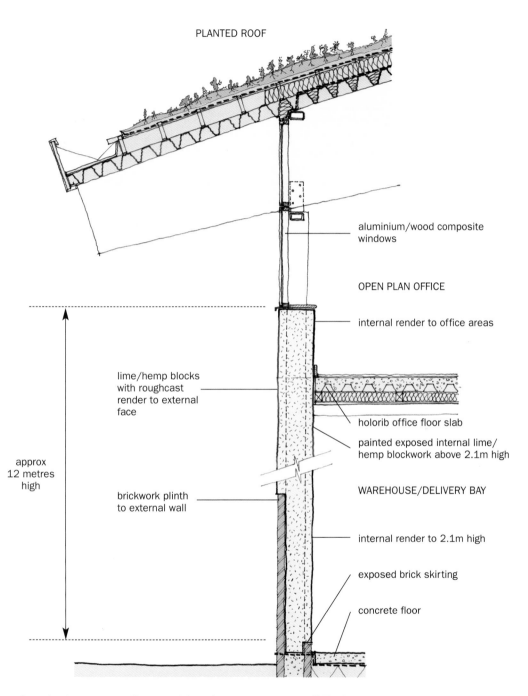

PLANTED ROOF

aluminium/wood composite
windows

OPEN PLAN OFFICE

internal render to office areas

lime/hemp blocks
with roughcast
render to external
face

holorib office floor slab

painted exposed internal lime/
hemp blockwork above 2.1m high

approx
12 metres
high

WAREHOUSE/DELIVERY BAY

brickwork plinth
to external wall

internal render to 2.1m high

exposed brick skirting

concrete floor

*Section through a hempcrete wall proposed for Adnams Brewery in Suffolk; there is a section
of brickwork at the lower external part of the wall; the wall will be 500mm thick, made
up of two courses of hemp block and a hempcrete mix between and around steel columns.
(Drawing: Aukett Fitzroy Robinson Architects)*

Drawing of a hemp-block house being constructed in the USA.

between the two walls of blocks. In this case the client has opted for an ecological form of building in preference to the normal steel and poly-iso insulation solution.

Hemp blocks have also been used to construct houses, but there seem to be few advantages over

casting hempcrete on site. However, if block making becomes established commercially, this form of hemp construction may become more competitive.

HEMP PLASTER

Normally, hemp walls are finished with lime-sand plasters or render, although it is possible to incorporate hemp in this as well. Hemp-lime plaster has also been used to finish a straw-bale building because the hemp gives added strength to the mix. Hemp-lime plaster can also be used as a plaster on conventional walls, such as concrete blocks, brick and stone. A normal hempcrete mix may be applied to the wall by either gloved hand or a float, or it can be cast against the wall by using shuttering. The resulting plaster will give a little insulation and will provide a warm finish to the wall. As long as the walls do not become saturated, the hemp-lime plaster should be able to cope with some dampness in old walls without damage, but it is important that the plaster can dry out properly. A number of tourism projects, where old stone cottages are being renovated, are employing a

Lime-rendered hemp wall. (Photo: Henry Thompson)

A 23cm (9in) solid brick wall plastered internally with hemp and lime, near Leominster.

hemp and lime plaster. Sand and cement or gypsum plasters on old walls may be very cold and attract condensation.

DETAILING

The design and detailing of hempcrete should present no particular problems to a good architect. It is important to detail window-sills and openings to ensure that there is good protection from driving rain, but there is no particular need for a large over-hang, as with cob or rammed earth walls. Hempcrete creates the possibility of a good air-tight construction since it can be pushed into every crevice so that there is a solid, unbroken mass of material. But it is important to ensure that, where a timber frame is used, cold bridging with the timber is avoided, particularly at the heads of walls. Hempcrete walls can be built on conventional foundations or can be part of a timber-frame post and beam construction where the floor is off the ground.

The positioning of the timber frame is a design decision and depends on the external finish and whether the timber frame is to be left exposed internally as grounds for fixing. If an internal lining board is used as permanent shuttering, this will also change the detail. In some cases it may be decided to use a rain screen cladding, such as timber boarding, and this will mean that the timber frame is moved to the outside of the hempcrete wall.

HEMP-LIME ROOFS AND FLOORS

In France there are a number of projects where a solid roof with internal permanent shuttering and hempcrete sprayed between the rafters has been cast. This form of construction is dependent on having a very light mix with a higher proportion of hemp to get good insulation and not to overload the structure. It should not be attempted by hand because this is practicable only with spraying. Hempcrete can also be cast as a solid floor instead of concrete. It can serve as a screed and is ideal for underfloor heating. Tiles can be laid on top of it, bedded in lime. This provides an ecological solution for insulated floors without the need to use a material such as polystyrene.

139

A hemp-lime plastered wall in an historic building that has been renovated in Chalons-en-Champagne, France.

USING LOOSE HEMP

I have come across one case where someone has used loose hemp for insulation in a floor. The hemp had apparently been allowed to get slightly damp and became infested with paper lice. A similar problem could occur if loose hemp were used as insulation in a roof. Most natural and cellulose materials if allowed to get damp can breed paper lice, which, while having no serious health effects, can be a nuisance. It is also possible that some people might be allergic to them. Loose hemp can be a fire hazard and, while it is not easy to burn, it would not be safe to use in this way.

HEMP AND EARTH

Mixing hemp and lime to make hempcrete is a tried and tested technique in France. Others have tried mixing hemp with cement but this produces a heavy composite with very little insulation value. It is possible, however, that the hemp reinforcement

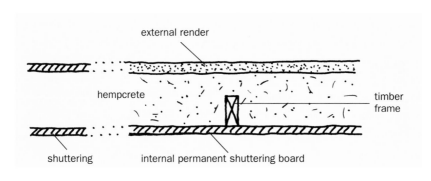

Plan of a hemp wall around a timber frame where the hemp is cast against permanent shuttering on the inside.

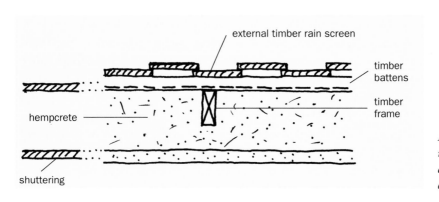

Plan of a hemp wall with an external rain screen of timber.

A roof being filled with hemp and lime insulation. (Photo: Henry Thompson)

A floor being cast with hempcrete. (Photo: Henry Thompson)

A test block of hemp and clay when first cast.

The same test block when dry; this block proved to be denser than a hemp and lime mix with similar proportions; experiments are continuing to get a better standard of insulation.

Experiments in County Leitrim with hemp and lime and hemp and earth; the hemp and earth is cast around forest thinning timber.

of concrete using cement may have some uses. It is also possible to mix hemp with earth, creating an alternative to rammed earth, cob or light clay, as has been discussed earlier. A house has been successfully built in Canada using hemp and earth, mixing hemp with a clay-rich sub-soil. The process of mixing the earth and hemp is the same as with lime, but even less water should be added. The mix takes a long time to dry out but it eventually turns to a very hard material, almost like stone. As with hemp and lime, the denser the mix, the poorer the insulation, but the attraction of this solution is the use of zero-carbon and zero-emission materials.

SOURCES OF SUPPLY

Because building with hemp and lime or earth is a relatively new idea, there is as yet no established supply chain. Since the process involves mixing lime and hemp, it may be necessary to obtain materials from separate suppliers, but it is only a matter of time before ecological builders' merchants will have hemp and lime readily available. Because this form of construction could so easily be adopted by the mainstream construction industry, codes of practice and guidelines will need to be prepared to ensure that builders use the materials correctly. These guidelines will also be useful to self-builders. The French hemp construction association provides training courses and these are likely to be offered in the United Kingdom as well. As with straw-bale or earth construction, it is important to get good hands-on training before embarking on the use of the materials as a self-builder.

Lime is readily available, but the special sort developed for use with hemp is not yet stocked in the United Kingdom, but will be shortly. Some of the French companies working in hemp and lime are now part of the multinational Lhoist group, which is based in Buxton, in Derbyshire. A number of specialist lime companies, such as Limetec, have invested strongly in developing hempcrete technology and have been working with Bath University to test mixes and methods.

142

Hemp can be obtained from a number of sources, mostly imported from mainland Europe, but the main producer of hemp in England, Hemcore Ltd, is based in Essex. Hemcore hemp has been used in a number of experimental building projects in Ireland. There are a few small builders who have developed expertise with hemp and offer a specialist service. The Old Builders Company in County Tipperary, Ireland, has been particularly active and has published many pictures of hemp building in progress on their web site.

THE PROPERTIES OF HEMPCRETE

Thermal Performance
Until more research has been done, it is not possible to give a conclusive evaluation of this. There is little doubt that buildings using hempcrete can be very airtight and thus more efficient; however, to establish clear measures of thermal resistance has not been easy. Some work was done by the Building Research Establishment for the Suffolk Housing Association hemp houses at Haverhill. According to the BRE, lime-hemp walls have a thermal conductivity of $0.12W/m^2K$ at 23°C. For a 300mm wall this should give a U-value of $0.2W/m^2/K$. It is has been argued by Ralph Carpenter, of Modece Architects, and others, that the U-value is not a good way to assess the thermal performance of this type of material. The actual thermal performance could be in excess of what would be expected of a synthetic/lightweight material with an equivalent U-value because of its high thermal retention properties. Most conventional insulants are lightweight with negligible thermal mass.

Interstitial Condensation
There are no available English data on the performance of a lime-hemp wall in this regard, but measurements have been carried out in France. Empirical evidence suggests that the high capillarity of the binder and the good water-vapour permeability should counteract any interstitial condensation problems.

Fire
When hemp is mixed with lime it becomes fire-resistant. Tests have shown that the hemp-lime is 'non-combustible' and has been tested to a temperature of 1,800°C for 4hr by the French Centre Scientifique et Technique et Bâtiment (CSTB).

Infestation
The hemp itself does not attract mice or rats because it is not a food source, added to which the lime binder is unpalatable and has been used throughout history to maintain levels of hygiene. Lime has a high pH value and is mildly antiseptic. Empirical evidence from historic buildings shows that lime is a good medium in which to preserve plant fibres and protect them from infestation.

Fixings and Solidity
Once the walls have fully hardened, it is possible to fix into hemp-lime walls direct. The timber studs provide more substantial fixing points and in a kitchen the studs should be left exposed for installing kitchen cabinets and other fittings; tiling may then be placed over the hemp-lime and timber studs. The walls become hard and are relatively strong compared with plasterboard dry lining or timber rain-screen. Once rendered with lime, the external walls would appear to be the same as conventionally rendered, concrete block walls to any passing vandal.

Services
Electrical services can be cast into hempcrete walls without difficulty, although it is best to use conduit for this. Other services can also be cast into or pass through the walls without difficulty.

FREE-STANDING WALLS –
THE CHELSEA GARDEN

It seems possible that hemp-lime walls can be constructed to be free-standing if a good frame is used. It is also possible to make prefabricated sections and move them, but with care, although there will be a danger of cracking if the panels are knocked in transit. A free-standing, hemp-lime wall was constructed at the Chelsea Flower Show in 2004 as part of an ecological garden designed by Celia Spouncer with children from Cedar Integrated Primary School in County Down. Constructed by The Old Builders Company, with support from Hemcore, Limetec and

Timber frame with wire mesh used for a hemp wall at the Chelsea Flower Show, 2004. (Photo: Celia Spouncer)

BELOW: Hemp wall at the Chelsea Flower Show complete. (Photo: Celia Spouncer)

Defra, the garden won a silver gilt award and introduced the idea of hemp construction to many visitors. The wall had to be constructed in a short space of time and, despite the fact that hempcrete is slow to go off, it was ready in time for the show. Handmade tiles and other features were incorporated in it, which also hints at some of the sculptural possibilities. Chicken wire was used to reinforce the walls because of the speed of its erection, but this would not necessarily be needed if there were more time.

IN CONCLUSION

At a pragmatic level, the viability of hempcrete construction has been proven. It is a simple and robust technology with some reasonable evidence of durability from the projects already built. The Building Research Establishment has raised no major concerns in its three reports on the subject and the Suffolk Housing Society is apparently happy enough to embark on another hemp building project. There was little difficulty in obtaining structural insurance cover for the Haverhill houses and mainstream building insurance companies have expressed interest. Hempcrete provides a solution to the need for more energy-efficient forms of construction that are low-carbon, made in part from renewable materials that are non-toxic, healthy, breathable, robust and simple to erect. Construction using lime-hemp composites offers the potential for up to 30 per cent carbon sequestration, that is, up to 30 per cent of the mass of the wall is locked-in, atmospheric carbon dioxide. This could be equivalent to 20 tonnes in a typical house. Dry plant material weighing 1kg typically absorbs 1.7kg of carbon dioxide in its production, so the use of plant material in the construction of our buildings contributes to carbon sequestration and reduces the emissions of atmospheric carbon dioxide.

Chelsea hemp wall after planting. (Photo: Celia Spouncer)

CHAPTER 8

Natural Insulation Materials

ENERGY EFFICIENCY A PRIORITY

Better insulated buildings will become essential in the future, but every architect, specifier and building owner is faced with a stark choice between environmentally-negative insulations and natural products. It is necessary to discuss natural insulation in the wider context.

The Value of Insulation

The need for greater levels of insulation to ensure higher standards in buildings is widely recognized. If we insulate our buildings well, then we can save money by reducing heating costs and also help to reduce carbon dioxide and other greenhouse gas emissions which are alleged to cause global warming. Climate change may lead to greater extremes of temperature and insulation is needed in hotter conditions to keep buildings cool, as well as in colder conditions to keep them warm. Despite the fact that to increase the insulation in buildings is a relatively cheap and economical solution to energy efficiency, a surprisingly high number of people do not insulate their homes and workplaces well. Extra insulation is one of the first things to go when cost cutting takes place, especially if someone else has to pay the heating or air conditioning bills in the future.

Insulation is much more important and cost effective than fancy pieces of renewable energy equipment. However, many people, when building or renovating their houses, are easily influenced by salesmen offering expensive, ground-source heat pumps, underfloor heating, solar panels and wind turbines. While these can be effective and appropriate in many

situations, it does not make sense to install such high-tech gadgetry until buildings are super insulated. Insulation and air-tightness have a far speedier pay-back than any expensive pieces of kit. The priority should be to reduce energy consumption first and then to look at alternative ways of generating energy.

But any insulation salesman will tell you that the average householder would be happy to spend £2,000 on a wide-screen television but not spend £1,000 on extra insulation; £1,000 on extra insulation will pay back in five to ten years and so provides an enormous advantage. We waste huge amounts of energy and this has led to a revival of interest in building nuclear power stations in an effort to generate more energy without further carbon emissions. However, the cost of building one nuclear power station would be sufficient to insulate every house in the United Kingdom and governments will have to decide which is the easier and better option.

It is usually quite easy to install a high standard of insulation in a new building, but it may be difficult to add insulation to existing buildings without having to change the general fabric. Dry lining the inside of walls can make rooms significantly smaller and lead to condensation problems. Despite this, installing insulation has to be a priority for society, particularly as so many people live in fuel poverty and cannot afford to pay for heating. Current government policy has been focused on installing central heating into the houses of the poor, even though many will not be able to afford the consequential bills as oil and gas prices rocket. Far less effort is going into insulating houses.

A decommissioned nuclear power station in North Wales; using low-impact insulation is a better and safer option to nuclear energy.

Legislation

Legislation is now forcing higher standards of insulation and is fundamentally altering the approach to building construction. Building regulations in the United Kingdom and Ireland are requiring higher and higher standards of thermal performance and these will no longer be assessed on an 'elemental' system, where it is necessary only to calculate the U-values for each element of a building – floors, walls, roofs and windows. Instead, a holistic analysis of the building, including heating systems, will assess its likely carbon emissions; while this allows for some trade-offs, it means that insulation standards will have to be much better.

The old standards equivalent to 60mm of insulation in a cavity wall and 150mm in a roof will now have to be replaced with at least 100mm in walls and up to 300mm in roofs. Along with more efficient heating systems, this is intended to create a 25 per cent carbon saving for each building. Furthermore, the performance of buildings once constructed must be checked. The EU Energy Performance of Buildings Directive requires all member states to introduce energy-labelling systems for certain building types. Consumers will be familiar with environmental labelling on refrigerators and washing machines, but this will also be in force for buildings eventually. 'Energy police' may even be able to call at random and carry out air-tightness and other checks to see whether a building complies! This brave new world of energy efficiency will come as a shock to developers and building companies who have hitherto been able to get away with buildings that were poorly insulated and often performed in practice much worse than had been predicted.

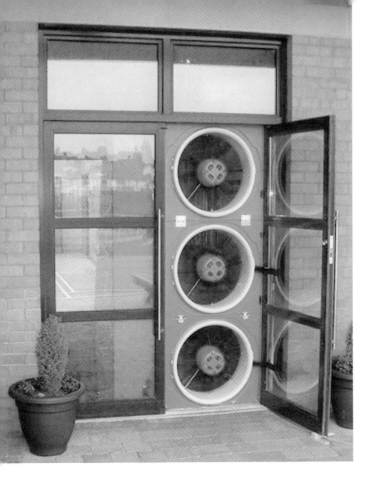

The three fans fitted in a door opening are pressurizing a school building in north Belfast in an airtightness test; this shows where air is leaking out, causing wastage of heat and draughts; these tests may be compulsory following the EU Energy Performance of Buildings Directive.

Furthermore, the home seller's pack for houses will include some energy performance data, and eventually all houses will have to be accompanied by information on fuel consumption and insulation standards. Market forces tend to have a diluting effect on the intentions to reduce carbon emissions, but gradually these pressures are beginning to have an effect. If the average homeowner or facilities manager had access to a thermal imaging camera, he could simply point it at his building and see where the energy was leaking out.

For many professionals, any sort of insulation material is a good thing if it saves energy and will help to comply with the new regulations. However,

many common forms of insulation are made from petrochemicals and involve the use of substantial amounts of energy in their manufacture. For environmentalists, this is somewhat contradictory, but, in addition, most synthetic insulations contain a wide range of additives that pose health and environmental risks. There is a confusing plethora of products, even from the same companies. Some fossil-fuel-based insulations use the prefix 'Eco' in their title, even though it is hard to see any ecological aspects to the material. I have heard polystyrene insulation promoted as an ecological product because naturally occurring styrenes are supposedly found in fruit such as strawberries. If it is necessary to select a synthetic insulation, for reasons of cost or practicality, it is a question of choosing the least bad and ensuring that it is appropriate for the construction system being used; there is little point in designing a building with the idea of having breathing walls and then using a non-permeable insulation. It is also better to avoid those products where there are health concerns, thus the Green Building Store claims on its website that, 'glass or mineral quilts produce minute fibres, which irritate the skin as you will know if you have ever installed them! ... There are suggestions that they may increase the risk of skin and lung cancers ... where contact is inevitable, wear a high quality respirator and full protective clothing.' Synthetic boards have little risk associated with them from casual handling, but they may damage the environment in other ways. The precautionary principle leads to the conclusion that synthetic insulations should be used only when there is no ecological alternative, but for many people it will still simply be a question of cost.

The introduction of stricter energy standards, while urged by environmentalists, will also present a challenge for the natural building movement because synthetic, hi-tech insulants may appear to have a higher performance and provide an easy-fix way to meet new standards. While some construction methods, such as cob or rammed earth which have relatively poor insulation qualities, can comply with the regulations by trading off against other elements, this may become harder and harder to do. But simply to substitute natural insulation for synthetic may also lead to problems in complying with regulations. The

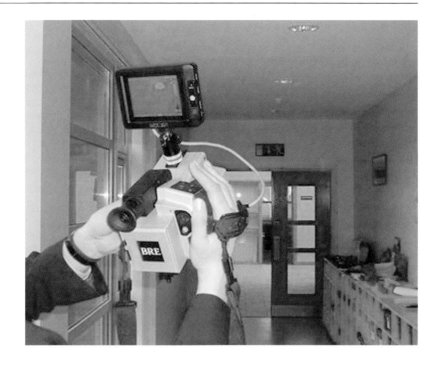

A thermal imaging camera will immediately show where energy leakages occur. (Courtesy: Building Research Establishment)

big synthetic insulation companies, which are now part of huge, multinational conglomerates who manufacture cement, bricks and concrete, have vast resources and are able to provide technical back up, free SAP (standard assessment) calculations and a range of impressive-looking publicity about the alleged environmental benefits of their products. It will require huge investment for natural insulation companies to compete with this so that they can demonstrate that their products perform as well or better as the synthetic ones.

On the other hand, most natural insulations are not always completely natural and, as we have suggested elsewhere, it is best to be pragmatic. Many natural builders will use materials such as polystyrene for underfloor insulation, since some natural products are not appropriate for this. There are large quantities of second-hand polystyrene available but these are not always easy to obtain when needed or in the right form. The natural builder will also have to make a choice between ecological, solid-wall forms of construction and timber frame, which will require insulation quilts and batts. These issues are therefore also discussed in other chapters.

NATURAL INSULATING MATERIALS

The following table lists common insulation materials and raises a number of issues and questions about them. The synthetic insulation industry is very quick to come to the defence of their products and the following notes are written defensively to avoid complaints from manufacturers. However, it is interesting to note that some of the leading manufacturers of synthetic insulation products have now begun to market natural insulations as well. Saint-Gobain, one of the biggest building materials producers in the world, sells insulation materials worth £2 billion per annum in Europe alone. As one of the main manufacturers of glass fibre, it is now offering a hemp insulation product. As society becomes more environmentally aware and oil becomes more expensive, there is little doubt that natural insulation products will become more widely used although they are currently three to four times more expensive than their synthetic alternatives. Just as consumer demand has driven supermarkets to sell organic produce, so many people may be willing to pay more for natural insulations, until they are more widely available.

Insulation Materials*

Synthetic or Conventional Insulations

Fibreglass	Fibreglass or glass wool is made from sand, limestone and borax. Materials are melted at a high temperature and spun into fibres. Formaldehyde resins are often added, together with water repellents.	Readily available and cheap.	Many building workers refuse to handle fibreglass unless fully gloved and masked. The fibres easily migrate throughout a building. Fibreglass has higher embodied energy than cement and also has life-cycle problems.
Mineral wool	Generally known as rockwool since it is made from volcanic rock into boards and quilts.	Readily available.	Has good fireproofing qualities but there are concerns about its health effects. Inert and will not degrade at end of life. Very high embodied energy. Manufacturers argue that it is a natural product because it is made from rock.
Expanded polystyrene (EPS)	Blown with substances such as pentane, a hydrocarbon and minor greenhouse gas.	Readily available. Made in slabs or as pellets and granules for blowing into cavities.	Only a danger in case of fire; there are also life-cycle and disposal issues. Builders should return all polystyrene waste for recycling. Suppliers do not always collect waste, but they can recycle the material.
Polyurethane foam	Other name is polyisocyanurate. Widely used in SIPS and other prefabricated products. Can achieve high level of insulation in foil-faced thin sheets.	Readily available.	Polyisocyanurates are volatile and can affect the health of workers in regular contact with them. Releases hydrogen cyanide if on fire and thus banned from use in furniture. Fire brigades have been concerned about fires in buildings containing some products. High embodied energy. Normal fire retardants are damaging to the ecosystem.
Multi-foils	A relatively new addition to the range of insulation materials. They consist of multiple layers of a metallized material interleaved with wadding and foams, typically up to a nominal 25mm thick.	Widely available, have featured on television and been used in some high-profile eco-buildings. Useful where thin material needed.	Independent testing suggests that the claims for high levels of insulation for these products are over-inflated. They have similar environmental problems to those indicated for foams and other synthetic products.

*The Carbon Trust is thanked for permission to use this table, which was prepared in a slightly different form for a Low Carbon Design Initiative Fact Sheet.

'Natural' or Ecological Insulations*

Cellulose and cellulose wool	Generally blown into timber frame, floors and ceilings. Made from recycled newsprint or other sources of cellulose. Product names: Warmcell, Homatherm, Vital, Ecocel.	Widely specified by green architects and builders in the UK and Ireland. German products available in quilts, semi-rigid batts and boards.	Can give good level of insulation, from largely recycled material. Heavily dosed with borate (low toxicity)-based fire retardant which is soluble in water. Requires only protection from dust during installation.
Wood fibre	Insulation batts and semi-rigid boards. Mostly bonded with natural resins: Homatherm, Thermosafe, Thermowall, Ultratherm, Pavatex, Pavatherm, Isolair, Diffutherm.	Mostly German, Swiss or Austrian but available from suppliers in the UK and Ireland.	Excellent low embodied energy product, could easily be manufactured in Ireland and UK but is currently not.
Sheep's wool	Made from natural wool with a variety of processes; Thermafleece, Second Nature, Ochre-wool, sheepwool.	Manufactured in the UK and Ireland, but do not assume that the wool has come from local sheep in all products.	Spun with polypropylene or other synthetic fibres and chemically-treated to protect against pests and for fire reasons.
Flax insulation	A range of quilts and batts made from a mixture of flax and other recycled and natural fibres; Flax 100, Natilin.	Mainly manufactured in other European countries such as Germany and Belgium.	Environmentally hard to beat, but not made in UK or Ireland, the original home of the flax industry. Normally some synthetic reinforcement is added.
Hemp insulation	A range of hemp insulation quilts and boards now available; Isonat, Florapan, Thermo-hemp.	Mainly manufactured in Germany and France.	At lease one hemp insulation product is made by the same company that makes fibreglass. It is claimed that hemp quilts perform to the same insulation standards as mineral wool. Some products contain virtually no synthetic chemical additives but may have synthetic reinforcement.

continued overleaf

* Note than some product names are given as examples but this is not a comprehensive list. Such names and contact addresses will change frequently and thus potential purchasers or specifiers are advised to contact the main supliers of these products.

Insulation Materials *continued*			
Expanded clay aggregate	This is a granular material made from clay which is expanded at high temperatures in a rotary kiln. Each granule has a hard ceramic shell with a honeycomb interior; Optiroc, Maxit.	Available from UK suppliers but may be made abroad.	An interesting alternative to insulating floors since it can be laid loose or in 15kg bags and replaces aggregate as well as insulation. Firing uses energy but the material does the job of several materials and is a natural product.
Cork	Bark of the cork tree; can be made into boards or used as granular fill, quite expensive, main use is in flat roofs.		A natural material and its use should support the continued sustainable management of cork forests in Portugal and elsewhere. The wine industry is replacing cork with plastic stoppers. Some cork products use environmentally unfriendly binders and additives.
Recycled cotton	Made from recycled denim and cotton fibres.	Imported from the USA but there are plans for manufacturing in the UK.	Appears to contain small amount of synthetic fibre reinforcement; uses phosphate-based fire retardant.

EXPANDED CLAY AGGREGATE

This is a product that is not well known and may be difficult to source. It is generally not marketed as a green product since it is widely used in mainstream building for non-ecological reasons. The fired clay granules are small brown pellets sold in 15kg sacks. They can be laid in the foundations of a building in place of both aggregate and insulation since they do both jobs. Builders use this product where it is difficult to use conventional aggregate. The material can be laid in the sacks or loose and can be pumped into place for large areas. There is no need for blinding. Screeds can be laid on top of it, but I could find no examples where a clay or earth floor had been cast on top. This material is of interest to natural builders because it is a natural, non-toxic alternative to materials such as polystyrene and poly-iso materials. Figures on insulation values and embodied energy were not obtainable, but the material is claimed to give a good standard of insulation. The firing will give a higher embodied energy

figure, but the replacement of heavy aggregate and the transporting and quarrying this would involve will reduce the overall environmental impact. A number of ecological builders' merchants stock the product.

NATURAL FIBRE QUILTS OF FLAX, COTTON AND HEMP

These three fibres are combined here because many of the natural insulation quilts currently available are often made from a mixture of them. The natural insulation industry is in its infancy and there is a constantly changing range of names and products. Most of the materials are three or four times as expensive as glassfibre or polystyrene, but, as production grows and oil prices rise, they are likely to become more competitive. A report by Impetus Consulting in 2002 described the potential of natural insulants, particularly the fibre-based, but admitted that few were commercially available. However, within the short subsequent period many competing materials have appeared on the market.

Flax and hemp insulation materials are made from the natural plant fibres. Known as 'non-wovens', they are frequently mixed in an attempt to create optimum insulation properties and strength, with the addition of cotton. An insulation material is now available which is made from second-hand cotton and denim. The use of recycled natural materials will be an important way to improve the environmental performance of such materials even more (*see* picture below).

Flax and hemp products are available in batts or rolls. As batts, they are reasonably rigid, which can be important in ensuring that they do not slump when installed vertically. Most natural insulation products use synthetic binding fibres that are generally low-impact or biodegradable biopolymers; some use polypropylene. It is difficult to get full information on the constituents of these products since the manufacturers have their trade secrets and most of the British companies are distributors who are sourcing the materials elsewhere in Europe. Normally the polymer fibres make up only about 2–8 per cent of the material. The published information on flax insulation states that it is bound with potato starch and that borax is added. Potato starch is a useful natural additive found in other natural insulation products.

Since natural insulation materials trap air, this contributes to their good insulating properties and

Flax insulation at Construction Resources; natural potato starch is added.

the manufacturing processes use much less energy and require no chemicals to foam the products or create air pockets in them. On the other hand, natural fibres need to be treated with chemicals such as borax in order to provide fire and insect protection. The products are non-irritating, not dusty and have no known health risks associated with them, either for the installers or the building's occupants.

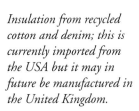

Insulation from recycled cotton and denim; this is currently imported from the USA but it may in future be manufactured in the United Kingdom.

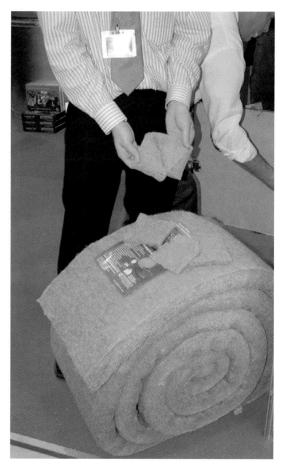

Hemp insulation in a timber frame with a proprietary breather membrane made from a low impact, PVC-free plastic.

Hemp insulation, supplied by Ecological Construction Products in Ireland but made in Germany; this quilt is made in layers so that it can easily be divided to suit whatever thickness is required.

Natural insulation products normally perform better in high humidity since they offer moisture control and are permeable to water vapour. Some natural insulations make it possible to dispense with synthetic vapour barriers, but it is important to check this with the suppliers. The natural fibre insulation quilts have limited heat storage properties, but because they behave differently from conventional synthetic insulations, the calculation of their thermal performance is different from synthetic materials, and this is discussed below.

SHEEP'S WOOL INSULATION

Insulation from wool has been successfully marketed by companies in Britain and Ireland and it has a natural appeal to ordinary consumers who are also aware of the difficult times faced by hill farmers. It is important, however, not to let the cuddly image of sheep's wool insulation obscure the fact that this is a relatively hi-tech product that performs as well as synthetic insulations. The wool has to be treated with some chemicals to protect it against infestation and make it fire-retardant, and it is usually bound with an acrylic solution. It is not necessary to use top quality wool and recycled material (shoddy) can be incorporated in the manufacturing process. It is best to ask questions like this of the suppliers and not assume that all branded products are the same. As with other natural fibre insulations, sheep's wool can absorb

Thermafleece wool insulation made in the United Kingdom, being installed in a roof. (Photo: Second Nature UK Ltd)

Thermafleece wool insulation installed in walls. (Photo: Second Nature UK Ltd)

Full-scale, cut-away model at Construction Resources, showing cellulose insulation in a wall and roof.

Cellulose insulation at Construction Resources may be either bought in bales or blown in by a specialist installer.

more than a third of its weight in moisture and release this without any damage to the material. There are no health problems associated with its handling and minimal health risks from very low levels of chemicals which might have been used on it.

Some natural builders have experimented with using untreated wool straight from the farm, but this is a high-risk strategy. Wool does not burn easily but chars, and may be relatively safe from the point of view of inflammability, but there will be a high risk of insect infestation. Such DIY solutions are only possible if the full hazards are understood and the installer is prepared to remove it if things go wrong. If in doubt, stick to the manufactured products.

CELLULOSE INSULATION

An insulation of choice for many years for greener architects, before wool and natural fibres became available, has been recycled newsprint and cellulose insulation that can be pumped into cavities by a registered installer or supplied in bags for loose fill. Some cellulose products are now available in batts as well. The insulation is sprayed in wet when this is preferred, and it is necessary to be fully masked for this process. There has been some criticism of the product for containing too high a proportion of borax and there is controversy concerning the mammalian toxicity of borax itself. While there are cellulose fibre products from Germany, the best-known product is made in Wales.

Semi-rigid cellulose batts are available from a range of manufacturers in Germany and Scandinavia. Some contain added viscose fibres and food-grade cellulose binders. Others are made with wood chippings and polyolefin fibres and some do not include chemicals such as boron-based compounds. Cellulose batts have very good acoustic insulation as well as thermal properties.

WOOD-FIBRE PRODUCTS

There are a growing number of wood-fibre products available as insulation batts and boards. These differ from cellulose products, which are made from wood fluff or recycled paper. In general, they are made from wood chips, recycled or virgin, and are bound with environmentally friendly binders. Some products are made from wood chips that are pulped, simply soaked in water and then pressed into boards and dried. Scientific work has been going on to extract natural resins and lignins which can bind such products, thus avoiding the toxic (such as formaldehyde) or synthetic, water-based glues, but pressed products may not necessarily require any binders or additives. Most wood-fibre boards do not provide a high level of insulation but they can contribute significantly if used in a warm roof detail in conjunction with other natural insulations.

Wood-fibre boards can be used as sarking on roofs as part of a natural building solution and are ideal for warm roof designs. The manufacturers claim that the normal, synthetic, breather waterproof membrane can be dispensed with and the sarking board used instead. This form of construction has been used in Scotland where traditionally sarking boards are used. The boards are strong enough to take some foot traffic over rafters during construc-tion and will withstand a certain amount of rain until they are covered. Some products are impregnated with latex to be moisture-resistant. Insulating wood-fibre boards can be used as external wall insulation, as a natural alternative to the usual synthetic systems and there are also mineral-based rendering systems, which can be applied over reinforcing mesh. Some boards are tongue and grooved as well and some woodchip boards are also used in Germany as underfloor and below-screed insulating applications.

There is much scope for the development of wood-fibre products since they can be used in a variety of ways to replace conventional synthetic and fossil-fuel-based materials. They often include a high level of forest by-product wood with no toxic additives.

OTHER AND LESS COMMON MATERIALS

A range of products is available made from different materials but which are currently less commonly used:

- coconut fibre mats are available and are mainly used for acoustic purposes

Pavatex wood-fibre boards that can be used as sarking boards on a roof; Swiss-made, this is a sophisticated product, which is widely used in its country of origin; the use of these boards does away with the need for a plastic breather membrane; the interlocking board is latex impregnated for moisture resistance, no glues or tapes are needed.

- rye grain pellets are used as an alternative to polystyrene balls
- jute is another fibre used for non-woven products similar to hemp and flax.

AUTOCLAVED, LIGHTWEIGHT BLOCKS

In mainland Europe, lightweight, autoclaved, aerated blocks have been used to improve energy efficiency. These are made from a mixture of cement and lime and require a foaming agent to produce air pockets. The best quality products are very light and can be easily sawn to give a very tight fit around openings. This is a quite different product from ordinary concrete blocks. Normally, aerated blocks are used in the United Kingdom as the inner leaf of a cavity wall, but they are used more efficiently as solid-wall construction, giving a high level of insulation. They are laid with very thin mortar beds and must then be rendered externally with a specialized reinforced polymer render. While this is not a particularly natural form of construction, it may be attractive to natural builders in some circumstances as aerated blocks are not quite as environmentally damaging as standard concrete blocks. Some of the companies manufacturing the blocks claim high environmental standards, particularly in terms of reducing waste and recycling and scrap material. They have also begun to experiment with incorporating natural fibres into the mix, although this may involve several more years of R&D before the products are brought to market.

AIR-TIGHTNESS, GOOD VENTILATION, BREATHABILITY AND THERMAL MASS

The science of insulation has been developed to measure the performance of synthetic products that are mostly lightweight and cannot absorb water. The construction industry is largely geared to the use of such products. Natural insulations, on the other hand, while they may also be lightweight, can absorb moisture, normally without damage, if properly installed in a building, and also have greater thermal mass, which slows down thermal transmission. But simply measuring the R value, the thermal resistivity of a material, does not give a complete picture of how it will perform if it includes thermal mass. In order to understand why natural insulations are much better for buildings and health it is important to understand the science of insulation.

Conventional building methods tend to use materials and forms of construction in which the 'breathability' of the materials and walls is not of great concern. Frequently buildings are plastered with cement and synthetic topcoat plasters and coated with synthetic plastic paints so that they are sealed against moisture permeability. Research into health problems in buildings, however, shows that one of the most worrying causes of respiratory illnesses is toxic mould. Where buildings are sealed and have poor ventilation, mould growth can flourish in cold, damp corners, often behind furniture where there is poor air movement. The mould spores can penetrate deep into the materials on the walls so that simple

washing does not eradicate them, it merely redistributes the spores around the house.

So serious is the potential health risk from this aspect of building construction that the insurance industry has been preparing for potential claims. Such claims are being pursued in the litigious USA, but such is the ignorance in the United Kingdom and Ireland that little has so far surfaced. Architects may also find a recent exclusion in their indemnity insurance policies stating that they will not be covered for claims relating to toxic mould. Such a limitation on risk means that green architects who state that their buildings are healthier, breathable and thus less at risk from toxic mould, may be excluded from doing so by their insurance policies.

In order for buildings to be energy efficient they must be air-tight, but this does not mean that they should not be well ventilated. Ventilation has to be carefully controlled so that draughts are excluded and air is allowed to come in and go out only as part of a designed system. There are now commercial passive ventilation systems on the market that can be designed into buildings. But many buildings are poorly designed and constructed so that holes and air gaps are left, often out of sight, allowing cold air into the building or heat to escape. Many windows and doors are poorly fitted or do not have good seals and thus a great deal of energy is wasted and discomfort results. The ventilation strategy often happens by accident rather than being designed in. The requirement in the building regulations for trickle vents in windows is meant to deal with this problem, but often people close off the vents thinking that they cause draughts.

It is important not to be confused about breathability as a concept – it does not mean air passing through the building fabric. Essentially breathability means that water vapour can pass through a material and thus it is important to know the vapour resistance of products and materials. The following table gives 'g values' (the resistivity multiplied by the thickness).

The basic principle of breathing wall design is to ensure that the wall becomes more permeable towards the outside. The highest resistance should be on the inside. In conventionally constructed walls, build-ups are the opposite of this, with very dense

Resistivity of Materials*	
Examples	**Construction resistance (g)**
air	5
cement plaster	2
lime plaster	1.5
clay plaster	0.8
gypsum plaster	1
cast concrete, depending on strength	6–50
foamed concrete	3.5
bricks	5
foil-backed gypsum boards	60
clay boards	1.8
extruded polystyrene	50
polyurethane foam	15
flax, wool insulations	0.6

* Extracted from a longer list, with the kind permission of Neil May, Natural Building Technologies.

and non-permeable materials on the outside, thus trapping moisture inside the building or building fabric. Breathability is related to the porosity of a material, but it is also important to understand the importance of hygroscopicity. To quote Neil May:

Hygroscopicity is the capacity of a material to absorb and release water as a gas (water vapour) from and to the air as the relative humidity of the air changes. The effect of materials with good hygroscopic capacity can be to stabilize indoor air humidity, to reduce surface condensation and, in certain situations, to slow down or accelerate the transfer of moisture through structures (depending on where in the structure the hygroscopic materials are situated). The consequences of this for design of insulation, vapour control and ventilation in both new build and in refurbishment are potentially huge.

Some materials will absorb and let out water vapour as the temperature and the humidity change. These materials are described as having hygroscopic qualities. Many building materials are unable to do this. The mass of a material will affect the amount of moisture that can be held in it and some will absorb water vapour more quickly than others. The relative humidity of a room will be more important than its temperature and it is often humidity rather than temperature that will affect the occupants' feelings of comfort.

Where naturally hygroscopic materials can help to regulate humidity, this can contribute to both energy efficiency and comfort. This is known as 'humidity buffering' and is an exciting concept for natural builders and the suppliers of natural building materials. Humidity buffering is a benefit of natural insulation to some extent, but even more for solid-wall constructions such as earth and hemp and lime discussed elsewhere. As a result, natural materials can help to provide greater comfort in buildings, reducing the need to call on energy-consuming solutions such as heating and air conditioning. These benefits are not recognized in regulatory systems which simply rely on crude U values, and thus designers of natural buildings may struggle with the regulatory and assessment systems which may predict a poorer performance for a natural material than would actually apply in practice. Buildings made of materials that are not responsive in this way will be less comfortable and will lead to the occupants' trying to regulate their environment by turning up the heating or opening windows.

Capillarity is a third important issue, which explains the draw of the material and thus its ability to absorb moisture. Some materials have a low capillarity, such as mineral wool, but if it does get very wet, it is slow to dry out. It is important to understand how 'vapour-open' materials can be, in addition to their hygroscopic capacity and capillarity. Synthetic insulations are generally inert and not as breathable as natural materials that are much more open to moisture movement. Natural insulations generally dry quicker because of this, provided that they are in a situation where they are not being constantly soaked.

Many conventional builders will be suspicious of natural insulating materials because there is an in-built prejudice and assumption that they are more prone to rot and decay and will not last as long. This is reinforced by experience of materials such as strawboard being used in inappropriate ways in

159

non-breathing construction systems. If a natural material gets wet and is unable to dry out it will rot. Interstitial condensation is also a great fear in building construction because it can occur, by its nature, in situations where it cannot be seen. But all these prejudices come from the use of conventional materials. The use of natural materials, particularly insulations, involves a complete mind shift in how buildings are designed and constructed based on a different approach to building science. Breathable materials must be used in breathable buildings with breathable finishes.

A simple box that uses a light source for heat and a temperature gauge at Natural Building Technologies; it is possible to see the time lag (or decrement) with insulation materials which have some thermal mass or delay; synthetic, lightweight insulation materials have no delay and also are ineffective in terms of moisture buffering.

How Insulation Functions

Insulation can resist heat flow through material in several ways:

- reflecting radiant heat
- resisting the conduction of heat
- preventing the conduction of heat; usually through what is known as thermal bridging.

Anyone with a simple technical knowledge of building science or even GCSE physics will understand these concepts, but what is frequently ignored is the issue of 'capacitive insulation', the ability of thermal mass to delay the flow of heat. In order to predict and understand how a building will perform thermally it is necessary to understand and to measure periodic heat flows. Solid material, such as a brick wall, concrete or rammed earth, will absorb heat and take some time before it transmits it. A much less dense material, such as polystyrene insulation, will behave quite differently. The dynamic properties of buildings can be measured in terms of time lag, admittance and what is known as the 'decrement factor'. It depends on the material, the thickness of layers and the sequence of layers in relation to the direction of the heat flow. The application of these concepts involves measuring the variation of temperature throughout a 24hr-cycle and gives a very different picture of the performance of insulation materials. To simply rely on U values or various thermal programmes which assume a steady state, gives a misleading picture. Of course, the simplification is there because the mathematics involved in assessing decrement are quite complex.

Some natural insulation materials such as wood-fibre have a slower time lag and materials such as cob, rammed earth and hemp and lime solid walls have substantial thermal mass; this means that they can even out thermal fluctuations and create a more comfortable environment. This is particularly important where passive solar gains are being employed in a design and where thermal mass is required to store heat. Dynamic factors such as thermal mass, passive gain and decrement must be understood and calculated in order to create an efficient building. The selection of building systems and insulation materials must be made in this context instead of by simply relying on the crude simplicity of systems currently in use. For those who do not want to get involved in complex mathematics the basic principles are actually quite simple to understand. The use of a combination of breathable, hygroscopic materials that have a thermal time delay is likely to result in a more comfortable, healthier building.

CHAPTER 9

Paints and Finishes

WHAT ARE NATURAL PAINTS AND FINISHES?

The issue of what constitutes a natural paint can be controversial and, as environmentally friendly products gain a greater market share, arguments between manufacturers as to whose product is more or less natural will become more common. A short conversation with someone selling a particular natural paint will soon lead to an explanation that only *their* product is natural. Unlike organic food, which is certified by the Soil Association, there is no generally accepted certification for natural paints. Attempts have been made by the European Union to organize an Eco label for paints, but this has been fraught with difficulties. However, to meet a growing demand from ordinary consumers, rather than the construction industry, a natural paint industry has grown up. This demand from the public is due to anxiety about the dangers and negative health effects of conventional paints and finishes. Thus in order to understand natural paints it is necessary to examine the problems with conventional paints.

For many years we have painted the timber, metal and walls in our buildings with a range of materials, many of which have been highly toxic and damaging to the environment. Famous characters in history are thought to have died from poisoning from the arsenic used in decorative materials. Lead poisoning from paints was also commonplace and lead was banned because of the brain damage it caused. Even today great care has to be taken in stripping paint in

OPPOSITE: Lime plaster finish to Michael Buck's cob building in Oxfordshire.

old buildings because of its high lead content. In more recent times conventional paints have had a high solvent content and have largely been synthesized from fossil fuels. Demand from the public for a wide range of colours and opacity in paints has led to the use of a wide range of chemicals, the most common of which, titanium dioxide (used to make brilliant white paints but present in coloured paints as well), is generally accepted to be environmentally damaging. Other materials, such as wallpapers, contain vinyl and are treated with fungicides, as are glues and pastes. Some finishes contain fire-retardant chemicals, which are not only toxic to people but are recognized to be particularly damaging to the wider environment, appearing in seals and polar bears in the Arctic. Paint strippers and other materials used to remove old decorations can also be highly toxic and damaging.

INDOOR AIR QUALITY (IAQ)

As houses become more energy efficient and airtight, the concentrations of toxic chemicals within buildings become more serious in their impacts on human health. Many people have taken out old windows and replaced them with uPVC windows, often without trickle vents to provide ventilation. Then in an effort to save energy and reduce heat loss, where vents exist they are often blocked up and many people do not open their windows to ventilate their houses. Offices with air conditioning often make it impossible for workers to open windows and the problem of so-called 'sick building syndrome' is familiar to many, even if they are unaware of its causes.

In the USA and many European countries there has been a great deal of concern about indoor air quality and standards have been published by governmental agencies, and in some cases these are enforced in building, health and safety regulations. In the United Kingdom and Ireland these issues have been largely ignored, which may explain why these countries have the highest levels of IAQ-related health problems. According to a leading British expert, Stirling Howieson, 'the UK is only now considering issuing some guidance on five compounds [nitrogen oxide, carbon monoxide, formaldehyde, benzene and polycyclic aromatic hydrocarbons]. Guidance, however, does not constitute a standard, and it remains unlikely that regulations aimed at ensuring good air quality in residential buildings will be forthcoming.'

Indoor air quality is a complex issue and is a factor in the choice of the building and insulating materials referred to in previous chapters. However, conventional paints, adhesives and other indoor finishes emit a significant range of toxic chemicals into the environment. Most of these are identified as volatile organic compounds (VOCs), and while these can also be emitted by natural materials, they become a much more serious concern at high levels when emitted by the synthetic materials used inside buildings. Many paints contain solvents for ease of application and to aid drying; and while in the nineteenth century a building would be left with all the windows open for weeks to allow the building and finishes to dry out, today builders want paints and finishes to dry almost instantly for the occupants to move in as soon as possible.

The highest levels of toxic emissions occur when a building is newly completed or has been newly decorated, and it can take several weeks for these emissions to reduce. In the first few months of a newly decorated building, the occupants are breathing in a toxic cocktail of substances. Many people continue to be sensitive to these chemicals over longer periods and can become hypersensitive to quite low-level emissions.

Decorating for the New Baby

Of particular concern is the practice of decorating a nursery for the new baby coming home. A tiny infant is able to absorb toxic chemicals at much higher doses than an adult in relation to its body weight, with potential serious consequences later in life. To redecorate the nursery and fill it with VOCs and other emissions, which are at their most potent in the first few weeks following the decorating, and then leave a baby in what is often an overheated, poorly ventilated room is a very dangerous thing to do. While there is as yet no evidence of cot deaths being associated with decorative materials, there have been concerns about flame retardants in cot mattresses. However, there are also flame retardants in curtains, carpets and other furnishings, quite apart from the toxic glues, fungicides and other compounds in conventional paints. Pat Thomas, a campaigner against dangerous substances in the home, claims that, 'Levels of VOCs in personal air space are much higher at night – when the body should be resting and repairing – and much higher than those measured outdoors during the same period.'

Childhood asthma is a serious problem in the United Kingdom and Ireland, and, while there are many causes, poor indoor air quality, emissions from building materials and paints are contributory factors. It is hard to establish specific causal links between particular paints and health problems, but the evidence of an increasingly unhealthy indoor environment is growing. A recent epidemiological study of 7,000 children in the Bristol area reported in *The Times* showed a correlation between asthma and chemicals in the home, including paints and paint strippers:

The study shows a clear connection between persistent wheezing and use of a range of domestic chemicals, such as bleach, paint stripper, carpet cleaner and air freshener. The use of household cleaning products has soared in the past two decades: the market has grown by 60 per cent since 1994.

According to Thomas, in a major study carried out by the US Environmental Protection Agency in 1985 it was shown that the greatest health dangers were in the home, not outside it, and yet most current legislation is concerned with air pollution, not indoor air quality. Dichlorobenzene, a solvent used in air fresheners, was found in the urine of 96 per cent of the children tested in one American state. So do not use air fresheners to take away the smell of nasty VOCs!

The tabloids like to scare people and the *Daily Mail* carried a front-page story with the headline

'Poisoned in the womb'. This reported on a study by scientists at the University of Groningen in the Netherlands, which showed how mothers could pass chemicals accumulated in their bodies on to their babies. Some of the chemicals that were found at worrying levels included alkyphenols, bisphenol, brominated fire retardants, organochlorine pesticides, phthalates and many more. These chemicals can be found in building and decorative materials.

Unfortunately, scare stories can create anxiety and may cause almost as much illness as the toxic substances themselves, and it is important to remember that, in a well-ventilated house or workplace, concentrations of toxic substances can be dissipated by simply opening the windows (if they will open, of course). Furthermore, by adopting the precautionary principle and reducing the toxic compounds in our buildings and using breathable natural materials it should be possible to reduce the risks substantially.

ENVIRONMENTAL POLLUTION

If you are concerned to behave ethically and responsibly, then the effect of the paint industry on environmental pollution and carbon dioxide emissions must also be of concern. But the use and disposal of paints in DIY or contractor's hands is also serious – everyone who cleans a paintbrush in the sink and flushes away paints, solvents and cleaners is causing serious pollution problems. Half-used tins of toxic gloss paint are sitting in every garden shed and garage in the land, and, when disposed of, usually end up in the bin and as landfill. As the tins rust, the contents leach out into the ground.

A study carried out by the WWF involved taking blood samples from 155 volunteers throughout the United Kingdom. They found that everyone who was tested was contaminated by a cocktail of highly toxic chemicals that were, despite being banned in the 1970s, still present in the wider environment. Of particular concern were organochlorine pesticides, used in timber treatments and polybrominated diphenyl ether (PBDE) flame-retardants found in many furnishings and decorative elements. Despite these chemicals having been banned, people born

after the 1970s were still contaminated. Despite the significance of this study, it was still limited in scope in many ways so that it was not possible to tell how different individuals had accumulated the contaminants. In a Greenpeace study in 2003, cited by WWF, house dust was also found to be highly contaminated with chemicals.

HEALTH RISKS FOR PAINTERS

According to Construction Resources, professional decorators are particularly at risk from chemicals in synthetic paints, and they claim that the World Health Organization International Agency for Cancer Research says that painters are facing a 40 per cent increased chance of contracting cancer (although I have not been able to verify this source). Construction Resources also refer to 'solvent dementia', a condition recognized in Denmark. Professional painters tend to be quite conservative and want to use conventional paints, but they are often impressed at the immediate health benefits of using natural paints.

WATER-BASED PAINTS

Because of the concerns about VOCs and other emissions, the paint industry has been encouraged by governments and the European Union to reduce its use of solvents and to introduce so-called water-based products. These may not smell as bad as but it is dangerous to assume that they are any more environmentally friendly than existing products. *The Green Building Handbook* states that:

> Water-based emulsion can still contain up to 7 per cent solvent and most 'VOC-free' paints will still emit some VOCs, albeit in minute quantities, from the other petrochemicals in the paint. While more healthy for the paint user, even fully water-based synthetic paints are not environmentally friendly, as they require a range of detergents and emulsifiers to suspend or dissolve the resins and binders in the water. These tend to foam and cause bubbles so an anti-foam agent is added, which in turn causes problems further down the line which need correcting with yet more ingredients.

The Green Shop near Stroud, Gloucestershire, a supplier of a wide range of green paints and other ecological products.

Some of the paints on display at The Green Shop from 'Earth Born'.

ALTERNATIVE PAINTS AND DECORATIONS

Because of these concerns about the health and environmental impact problems of conventional synthetic paints, a wide range of natural decorative materials has been made available in an effort to offer alternatives. Of course, the term 'natural' can be misleading since substances used in the past, such as arsenic and lead, are naturally occurring. Thus it is important to check carefully when buying or specifying 'natural' paint how much information is provided

about the nature and manufacture of its contents. To rely simply on 'what it says on the tin' is not necessarily sufficient, and even product data sheets and health and safety (Control of Substances Hazardous to Health Regulations [COSHH]) sheets may not answer all your questions.

However, the development of natural paints with much lower levels of solvent and the use of natural materials creates the possibility of an indoor environment that is much less toxic. Many of the products that are now available also assist with the breathability of natural wall materials, can be more easily applied to other natural materials and provide a range of aesthetic options that are more natural in their appearance.

THE MAIN COMPONENTS OF PAINT

Paints consist of five main components:

- pigments
- binders
- solvents
- preservatives
- driers and anti-skim agents
- substances which assist flow and consistency in the tin.

When buying or specifying paints it is important to try to find out what each of these is made of and to compare the composition of 'natural' paints with conventional.

Binders are usually glues made from vinyls and acrylics. These are generally not regarded as a serious health risk. PVA glue and face paints (which are made from vinyls and acrylics) are widely used by children, but there are still health concerns with their manufacture. Some paints use methyl cellulose, which sounds like it might be nasty but is used as a laxative. Natural paints use dammar resin, linseed, castor and other natural oils. Natural oils still contain VOCs but these are less damaging.

Pigments may be natural or synthetic. They add colour and opacity to paint and the most common is titanium dioxide and can be found in many 'natural' paints. Titanium dioxide occurs naturally in ilmenite and rutile, very common in the earth's crust, but there are concerns about how this is being mined in often ecologically sensitive areas; 3.5 million tonnes of titanium dioxide minerals are mined every year. Neil May, of Natural Building Technologies, claims that synthetic oxides have less of a damaging environmental burden than natural oxides, but suppliers of natural paints, such as The Green Shop in Gloucestershire, advertise the availability of natural ochres, mined locally at Clearwell Caves in the Forest of Dean. It is possible to make up your own paints by using pigments supplied as powders and many of these will have been derived from the earth, but others may be synthetic.

Solvents in the past most commonly meant white spirit and turpentine, but these have now been removed or modified and restricted in use. Many paints are now water-based, but some natural paints use citrus and balsamic oils. Turpentine, which comes from the pine tree, can have serious health risks and is unlikely to be available, although many years ago 'turps' was freely used. Citrus thinners can adversely affect some people and so some natural paint companies use petrochemical products called isoaliphates as alternatives.

Driers, flow agents and other additives are less common in natural paints, but it is important to check whether the paints contain thickeners, surfactants, anti-foaming agents, driers, biocides, plasticizers or coalescing co-solvents.

Many additives in synthetic paints smell awful and the nose or smell test can be useful; if something smells bad, makes your eyes run or makes your throat dry then you may not want to use it. However, it is important to remember that natural paints – which generally smell better – are not entirely free of noxious substances either.

VOCs in paint most commonly come from organic solvents and can cause serious skin irritations. Toluene and xylene are common as they are derived from benzene; these chemicals can attack the central nervous system and the internal organs. However, VOCs are not just emitted by paints, they are a serious problem in air fresheners, deodorants and cometics (if you really want to give yourself a fright read the label on a bottle of conventional hair shampoo).

Preservatives are normally chlorine-based and are necessary to prevent paint from going off and toxic mould from forming. Preservatives are common in detergents and, even if they are not harming people, they are flushed down the drains in greater and greater quantities to damage the ground water. Ecological or natural paints should not use such harmful chemicals.

Traditional and 'heritage' paints should be treated with caution as some may contain synthetic substances necessary to replicate the paints of former days.

ALTERNATIVES

Mineral and silicate paints are inorganic paints made from minerals such as silicate clay and aluminium silicate. These kinds of paint react with the wall material that they are being applied to, such as a lime render, and acquire their binding quality through this reaction rather than the use of glues and binders. Silicate paints are generally breathable and less environmentally damaging and are therefore useful in natural building.

Casein wall paints can be made from dried Quark or milk curd, either from the manufacturers or you can try and make them yourself. A variety of mixtures of other oils and pigments can be added and the process is as much like cooking as making paint.

Lime wash and paints may be made by using lime. Good quality lime putty will give you the best results and natural pigments can be added to it. There are a number of suppliers of lime products around the United Kingdom and Ireland and they can advise on paint solutions. It is important to handle lime and lime powders with great care since lime is caustic; facemasks and eye protectors as well as gloves should be worn. However, once applied, lime is a natural biocide, does not emit any toxic chemicals and will help to keep buildings healthy and free from mould.

Earth paints – the use of the word earth in the names of some paints does not necessarily mean that they are made of the same materials as earth plasters. A typical 'earth' paint would, for example, be composed of water, some clays, chalk and kaolin. Earth paints have the claimed ability to absorb moisture and thus even out humidity in buildings.

Fields of flax, producing linseed oil, are a pleasant relief to bright yellow rape in the English countryside.

BIOFA is another natural paint product.

Auro Paints were one of the pioneers of natural paints.

LIVOS is yet another natural paint.

Oils, stains and varnishes may be derived from plants and natural resins. Linseed oil is one of the main ingredients in natural paints and a range of waxes and clear finishes. The oil comes from the crushing of flax seeds. It is thus a renewable material and a by-product of the growth of flax for linen manufacture and natural insulation products. Floor and furniture waxes can be made from beeswax, larch resin and essential and citrus oils. Floors get some of the roughest treatment in houses and it is worth experimenting with a small patch of wood before treating a large area; but natural oils and waxes tend to remain quite soft and will not necessarily tolerate heavy wear. Some of the more robust natural oils and waxes for floors may still contain some synthetic compounds and solvents such as aliphatics. Natural oils and varnishes are very good for wood as they penetrate into it more successfully than poly-urethane-type varnishes, and, while they will not give such a high gloss appearance, they do not make the wood look like plastic. Natural oils and varnishes for external use may contain metallic powders that act as filters to ultra-violet light.

There is a bewildering array of natural paint products, most of which originate in Germany and with names such as Auro, Livos, Biofa, Aglaia, Osmo, Holzweg and Earthborn. There are some products that appear to be British-made but which are imported and relabelled, and there are others which are made here. It is best to take the advice of an eco-builders' merchant, but if he avoids answering your questions about a particular product as to its constituents and origin then try somewhere else.

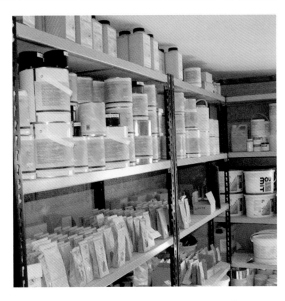

Natural Building Technologies have a range of trade paints and are developing their manufacture in Britain.

Clay plaster on display at Natural Building Technologies.

Clay plaster on reed boards at Construction Resources.

Suitable clay and earth on site can be simply screened and used as a plaster, mixed with sand and possibly gauged with lime.

Lime plaster finish to Michael Buck's cob building in Oxfordshire.

PAINT STRIPPERS AND CLEANERS

Many conventional paint strippers are dangerous, giving off toxic gases and must be disposed of as hazardous waste. However, there are also water-based strippers which are safer and, while they may require two or three coatings, work very effectively. There are also natural plant- and citrus-based thinners and cleaners, which are much more attractive than white spirit or turpentine substitutes.

CLAY PLASTERS AND FINISHES

Proprietary clay plasters are made from clay, sand and natural fibres such as straw. They can be used to give a smooth or textured finish and left in their natural state or painted with natural paints. Some textured plasters also come in a range of subtle colours. Clay plasters can be applied by hand in the normal way or sprayed; they are quite slow to dry out but have the advantage of being easy to repair. The plasters can be dampened and reworked without difficulty. They can be applied to most conventional materials such as gypsum plasterboard, but the natural building enthusiast may also wish to use wattles or reed boards and matting.

Proprietary clay plasters come in brown paper sacks and are quite expensive, but it is possible to make up your own; the method is similar to that described in Chapter 2. Clay, straw and sometimes sand are mixed together, and manure from cows or horses can also be added to give the mixture added flexibility. This can be slapped by hand on to wattles or hurdle. If you want something that is a little more sophisticated, then you can sift the plaster by using a screen and create a powder much like the bagged material. It will depend upon how much time and labour you have available.

Various additives can be combined with self-made earth plasters, such as lime, natural oils, cooked flour paste, casein or milk powder, alum, kelp or gum arabic. One book on the subject, by Guelberth and Chiras, also suggests cactus juice, not readily available in the United Kingdom or Ireland. It is important to be careful about the use of oils since they may not fully mix with the clay and behave differently in extremes of temperature.

Clay plaster on unfired earth bricks; architects: Arc Architects.

Coir carpet made from coconut fibre.

Linoleum, a traditional material, is making a comeback because of its natural characteristics.

Tiles that have been laid on a hempcrete floor.

Timber floor coated with a non-glossy, non-polyurethane, natural water-based varnish.

Clay plasters are ideal for use with natural building methods such as cob and straw-bale, but it is always important to experiment with a small area first. Clay plasters used externally should still be regarded as slightly high risk in a wet temperate climate and should not be seen as being as effective as a traditional lime plaster or render. There have been some external earth plaster failures, but internally as a decorative element there should be few problems if applied properly. (Lime renders and finishes are discussed in Chapter 6.)

FLOOR COVERINGS

There is a wide range of floor coverings made from natural materials that will compliment a natural building. While fired tiles consume a great amount of energy to produce, as do bricks, they may be an ideal finish for limecrete or clay sub-floors. Vinyl-based floor coverings should be avoided because of negative environmental impacts; traditional linoleum made from cork, jute, chalk and linseed oil is hard to beat. There is also a wide range of natural fibre mats and carpets made from reeds, coconut fibres and such like. Flooring installers will try to use a range of adhesives to stick or cement these materials to the floor. Where possible, lime, water-based adhesives or mechanical fixings should be used. There is little point in using a natural material and then fixing it to the floor with a toxic glue.

IN CONCLUSION

It is important to have different expectations of natural finishes. Natural paints and other materials cannot simply be substituted for conventional materials. For some architects and builders alternative products are unsatisfactory because they expect them to work in the same way as synthetic products. Their covering power may not be as good, and the results one day may differ from those the next. Drying out will take longer and colours may not be as strong, but, on the other hand, the natural look to the paints creates a very different aesthetic from synthetic paints. If you are looking for soft or luminescent finishes, these are better achieved with natural mixes. Sometimes finishes can be a little dusty and not washable like vinyl paints, and so it is necessary to understand the strengths and limitations of the product you want to use before choosing it. There may be a variable performance in terms of durability. As with other natural materials, they do a different job in a different way. But many proprietary natural paints are excellent and provide a better and longer lasting solution, especially when applied to natural materials.

CHAPTER 10

Planning, Regulations and Professional Advice

PROFESSIONAL ADVICE

The natural building movement includes a mixture of self-builders, enthusiasts, professionals, small construction firms and materials manufacturers and suppliers. Many of the people who have built some of the alternative buildings illustrated in this book are highly suspicious of professionals because they believe that they represent the status quo and would not understand the aims of natural building. There is a strong belief that natural building techniques liberate or empower ordinary people to create environments for themselves without being dependent on experts and the authorities.

Some of the buildings illustrated here have been or are being built without planning or building regulations approval. On the other hand, many of the best buildings have full approval and there has been support and encouragement from the authorities. Some projects have apparently been built without any input from professionals and yet nearly everyone has sought advice or help from friendly experts, books or Internet sites.

It is important to distinguish between expertise and professionalism. A number of the experts who have blazed the trail in natural building do not have professional qualifications or are only partly qualified, nevertheless, they have developed a significant level of expertise that puts them on a par with professionals. Indeed, many of the people involved are polymaths with expertise in design, building, materials science and alternative technology. Conventional professional disciplinary boundaries start to disappear when you get together a group of people involved in natural and ecological buildings. Despite this, there are those who deny the value and importance of expertise and professionalism, even when they have made use of this for their own projects.

If natural building is to be more widely adopted it may have to shrug off an image of amateur self-builders who feel that they can ignore the authorities and professionals. In reality, there is a significant need for much more expertise underpinned by research and science. But many middle-of-the-road professionals are highly suspicious, if not downright hostile, to natural building and this can create many problems for people who want to build natural buildings. This is a complicated issue because some of those who are attracted to natural building think that it can be done cheaply and without professional help. At which point they find that, when they try to build a house with a mortgage, the building society wants an architect's certificate; they have to get planning and building regulations approval and, without professional help, find this very difficult. But, because they are working on a low budget, they feel that they cannot afford the fees of architects, engineers and quantity surveyors, not to speak of planning consultants and natural building experts.

It is advisable for anyone undertaking a building project, of whatever size, using natural and innovative building materials that they seek good professional and expert help. Such help may not always come from a conventional professional but it is vitally important to check on the expertise of anyone advertising his services, whatever qualifications he may have. The best way to do this is to visit previous projects and to interview previous clients. It is not a good idea simply to rely on websites and general claims.

At the other end of the spectrum, clients who commission large and expensive buildings will suggest to their architects that they might include a few green materials, but often just for show, not as the central principle of the construction. Developers, public sector organizations and professionals are frequently not yet willing to embrace the principles of low impact construction fully, and cling on to many environmentally damaging technologies. Often these organizations will have complicated tendering procedures, largely restricted to big commercial undertakings, and the young up and coming alternative professionals have little chance of being appointed.

Organizations that Can Help

The mainstream professional bodies are unlikely to recommend architects or engineers with a specialized knowledge of natural building. It is necessary to seek out alternative organizations such as the Association of Environment Conscious Builders (AECB), the Scottish Environmental Design Association (SEDA) or the Environmental and Sustainable Construction Association (EASCA) in Ireland. These list professionals, builders and suppliers who are interested in green construction. Some local authorities work in partnership with The Green Register, to maintain a list of people who have undertaken some basic training in green building and this is developing on a regional basis. There are a number of environmental information and education centres throughout the United Kingdom and a handful of sustainable development and building trusts that will have good local contacts, such as in Somerset and Cornwall (*see* References). The Centre for Alternative Technology (CAT) in Wales runs a large number of training courses and provides a great deal of information. CAT also offers higher-level degree courses in collaboration with some universities on sustainable architecture and building.

Using the Best Expertise

There are great dangers in using the Internet as a source of knowledge and expertise. While there are some excellent websites, there are also unscrupulous people who offer dubious information, appearing to be experts but without anyone being able to check what they say. As a general rule, it is better to go to

organizations and sites that represent a wide range of people rather than those that are selling exclusive services. Many Internet sites originate in the USA with undisclosed locations and they may be promoting forms of construction that are appropriate in Arizona but not in Snowdonia.

Design is another problematic issue in that many self-builders think they can make a perfectly good job of designing their own building. Sometimes they may have artistic talents and are able to create something beautiful. But it is also important to respect what a good designer has to offer: to work with an architect can be a positive and fulfilling experience that can help people to achieve their dreams, way beyond what they first imagined. Unfortunately, architects have the reputation of being arrogant and egotistical, an image reinforced by the media and international superstar architects who design prestigious buildings. Sadly, not all architects are blessed with the skill of working in partnership with their clients, to be flexible and to listen without imposing their preconceived ideas. Many architects also remain surprisingly ignorant of green building principles and, despite attempts by the RIBA to introduce sustainability into the curricula of schools of architecture, the situation is only slowly improving. On the other hand, there are a growing number of architecture firms who are committed to environmental best practice and have some experience of using alternative and natural materials and construction methods and are willing to incorporate these into their designs.

Good green architects and natural building experts should bring a willingness to share in the creative design experience, and give good sound advice on the selection of building systems and materials. Ideally, this should save the client money, but there are many who thought they could do without experts and found it to be a costly mistake.

There are many beautiful, poetic, natural buildings, some designed both with and by architects and some without. Unfortunately, there are also green architects and experts who allow their obsessions with technology and energy efficiency to produce boring and uninspiring buildings. There are also some exciting buildings with innovative heating and insulation features that do not work very well. It is yet early days and there is bound to be a wide range of experiments that work and some that do not. We can all learn from our mistakes and it is important to share this experience. But such is the hostility to green building from some quarters that there is a tendency within the green building movement to be cautious about admitting to failure in case this is used to condemn the whole movement. Another danger is that well-intentioned self-builders who make a mess of things can do a lot of damage to those who come after. Prejudice and hostility to natural building can be stoked at a local level when buildings are not constructed properly and where there are failures and problems. Much needs to be done to establish a good working relationship between natural building enthusiasts, professionals and the suppliers of materials or services so that someone determined to embark on a really low-impact building project need not feel like an isolated pioneer or someone who will be taken advantage of.

PLANNING AND OTHER PERMISSIONS

There is a great deal of confusion about what approvals are required when a building project is initiated. Planning permission and building regulations approval must normally be sought. It is increasingly necessary to check matters with banks, building societies and insurance companies since all can potentially throw a spanner into the works where innovative natural building is concerned.

Planning approval is required except where a project falls into the category of 'permitted development'. A small shed, summerhouse or house extension may fall into this development category and many natural building experiments have come about in this way. Some agricultural buildings may not require approval. But even if planning permission is not required, other approvals may still be essential. Even temporary buildings may require planning permission, but there are circumstances where the authorities have turned a blind eye to some natural buildings in the belief that they will soon fall down or where no nuisance is being caused. It is better to assume that planning permission will be required and that there may be many restrictions, not just from general

planning policy, but from conservation areas, national parks and areas of outstanding natural beauty, and so on.

It is always best to try and work with planning officers when starting work on a project. To assume that they are hostile is not the right approach, as planning officials may help to find ways around what at first appear to be negative policies. There is an element of flexibility and subjective judgement in planning decisions, and to get officers and the local planning authority on your side is always the best strategy. On the other hand, it is not always a good idea to rush into the planning office at too early a stage, brimming with enthusiasm for a proposed straw-bale building or an eco-village without having worked out your proposals and tactics well in advance. Planning officers and other officials will want to be sure that you know what you are doing and that you will take a professional and responsible approach. Seeking advice from a sympathetic consultant at an early stage is a worthwhile thing to do. Working out your proposals carefully, but being flexible and willing to change and take on board suggestions, is also important. Be willing to go round and talk to neighbours, parish councillors and others. This will pay off in the long run if you can convince them that your proposal is responsible, attractive and not a new age hippie encampment!

It is important to construct your arguments carefully and to have facts and figures on the environmental benefits of the project, such as how much emitted carbon dioxide will be saved and how waste water is being treated on site. While being amenable and flexible, it is also important to be determined and willing to go all the way, if necessary, to appeals and public enquiries. Planning appeals and public enquiries are expensive and exhausting and should be avoided if at all possible.

If the principle of planning permission is established, then the intention to be a natural building should not cause a particular problem as planning policy and regulations do not specify how a building should be built, merely what it will look like. If a building is in harmony with the local vernacular and its setting then there should be no problem. Unfortunately, this can sometimes force the use of materials that are not environmentally friendly or as low-impact as might be desired. Timber cladding may be the best option as regards sustainability, but all the other buildings in the area may be made of brick. Problems like this should be anticipated at an early stage. It is important to remember that town and country planning ideas came from progressive people who wanted to protect the beauty of our towns and countryside and to encourage better environments for people, such as garden villages. While it might seem that planning favours the rapacious developer, we need to ensure that it also supports the natural builder.

Building Regulations

Building regulations are an important consideration in natural building. They are there to protect the health and safety of the occupants and without them there might be more collapses, building failures and fires. There is a built-in tendency to cut corners in building, especially where profit is concerned, and so the regulations are there to protect us all, even if they may seem overly bureaucratic and restrictive to the natural builder at times. In the future, building regulations will also attempt to encourage a more sustainable approach and we have an important job to do to ensure that natural building is seen as a way to achieve this.

The regulations rely heavily on codes of practice, technical guidance and standards, and if these are followed then there should not be too much of a problem. Regrettably, many natural building techniques do not have technical standards and thus fall into the discretionary powers of the local building control office. If refusal results then there is an appeals procedure, but, as with planning, it is better to get the building control officers on your side from the start. It may be necessary to work things out from first principles instead of using standard tables and this is where professional help may be crucial.

In most cases, building control officers are fascinated by a new challenge and, rather than being hostile, will do their best to find out more and to provide assistance. They operate a good network and will seek help and advice from other offices if they come across something unfamiliar. Straw-bale buildings have been approved in the United Kingdom on the basis of their compliance with the California Building

Codes and most of the forms of construction referred to here have been approved in at least one part of the country. Professionals undoubtedly come in useful in this process and the self builder will be an innocent abroad if he tries to submit proposals for a building made of natural materials without providing a full technical back-up. To find precedents elsewhere can be very useful since this can convince a sceptical official. Try taking him or her to visit another such building.

To comply with the energy regulations may not always be easy because of the dependence on U-values and SAP calculations. However, the regulations are changing to a more holistic approach to the reduction of the total carbon load for a building and this can work in favour of the natural builder, where trade-offs between different parts of a building can help to get approval for a thick cob wall which, in theory, does not meet the elemental U-values.

Some natural builders have turned to the 'approved inspector' route, which is a way of employing independent experts who will certify that a building complies with the regulations. However, this is essentially an insurance scheme and is based on an assessment of risk as well as whether best practice is being followed. To go through the discipline of submitting drawings to building control and getting regular local inspections is a valuable process and will help others following after.

The building regulations are being amended to require much higher energy efficiency standards and to introduce sustainability requirements. While this sounds as though it should support and favour natural building, with its inbuilt low-impact and low-carbon effects, this may not always be the case. If regulations and codes come into force which restrict the methods used, then the flexibility and experimentation of natural building may be impeded. Lobbying by commercial vested interests may try to force people to use expensive proprietary systems, outlawing handmade improvised local solutions.

INSURANCE

Insurance and certification may be a problem for natural builders. Bodies such as housing associations and education authorities are required to comply with official demands for structural insurance, and housing developers like to say that they have approval from such bodies as the National House Building Council (NHBC). These processes can be quite conservative in policy and accept only forms of construction with which they are familiar. Anything unusual involves hitting the panic button and may lead to problems. For instance, there are inbuilt prejudices against solid wall construction and this might result in opposition to hemp or earth walls. Here again it is important to start talking to the building insurance and certification bodies at an early stage and to bring them along. Agrément certificates will not always accompany natural building methods and materials and thus information about other successful projects must be assembled. On the other hand, some insurance companies have taken a particular interest in innovative methods of building and may be more helpful as a result.

Household insurance may also be a problem because unusual forms of construction are frequently penalized. However, owners of straw-bale, cob and thatched buildings have been able to get insurance from mainstream insurance companies. It is important to be honest in insurance declarations because if a building does suffer an unfortunate accident of some kind and the loss adjuster arrives to find that the building was not as described on the form, then the whole insurance may become invalid. Many owners of brick-clad, timber-frame houses will have ticked the box saying brick and masonry on their insurance proposal because they do not realize that there is a timber frame hidden inside and this may lead to problems in the future.

Natural builders may also run into problems with building societies and banks that rely on reports from surveyors who have a somewhat narrow and sometimes ignorant view of building. A correctly built cob wall that is naturally draining, and thus does not have a damp-proof course, may find that a surveyor is recommending the installation of an injected DPC. There are plenty of anecdotes about surveyors who did not notice that a wall was built from cob or straw as once it is properly rendered on the outside it could easily be made from concrete block or stone. Some straw-bale builders have described their buildings as

having cellulose insulation, which is scientifically true but somewhat misleading.

In practice, most natural buildings are no higher risk than conventional buildings. Some modern innovative forms of house construction involve light-weight steel frames coated with expanded polyisocyanurate insulation and are accompanied by BBA certificates and various warranties, but such buildings are likely to run into far more problems in the years to come than a well-built natural building. The construction industry is notorious for its ready acceptance of poor quality new technology, such as the heavy concrete system buildings of the 1960s and the 1970s and the British government is again encouraging prefabricated construction as a solution to the demands for low-cost housing. In this context, prejudice against genuinely low-impact building using materials and construction methods that have been in use for hundreds of years, seems somewhat misplaced.

NOTABLE PLANNING BATTLES

The Somerset Straw-Bale Battle

Despite the advice that it is important to work with the approvals system, some natural builders have run headlong into confrontation with the authorities and it is worth examining a couple of examples that highlight the issues. Caroline Barry is a woman who wanted to live an ecological life-style on her small-holding in Somerset, not far from Glastonbury. She found it impossible to get planning permission for a house on her site even though it was already occupied by several agricultural buildings of mixed quality. She came up against a complicated set of policies that are designed to prevent unattractive and unacceptable development in the countryside. However, the definition of a smallholding and what she was required to do to justify getting planning permission was too onerous for Caroline who was handicapped by illness and not able to earn a commercial living from the land. Despite this, she ran courses and inspired many local people to take up more ecological ways of living. She went ahead and built a small, single-storey, temporary house on her site using straw bales, because the caravan on her site was damp, unhealthy and hard to heat.

The Caroline Barry house in Somerset, subject to a lengthy planning battle.

The Tony Wrench roundhouse at Brithdir Mawr, in the Pembrokeshire Coast National Park; this low-impact dwelling has been the subject of a major planning struggle. (Photo: David Spero)

But building a low-energy, straw-bale house without permission led her into a twenty-year struggle with the authorities, which resulted in her gaining a conviction for non-compliance with an enforcement order. Anyone who reads the many hundreds of pages on this case will see that she ended up in a Kafka-esque web of red tape and bureaucratic intransigence, which was broken only after a planning appeal at which the inspector ruled that she had won her case on the basis of the human rights legislation.

She now has planning permission and is allowed to stay in her house, but only on the basis that it must be demolished or removed when she dies or moves away. In fact, at one stage in the long saga, she and a group of friends dismantled the house, drove it around the countryside on the back of a lorry for a day to comply with an enforcement notice to demolish it, and then re-erected it in a few days. This demonstrated the flexibility and demountability of a natural building using very simple technologies.

During the planning appeal an attempt was made to use the planning guidance which had been issued by the Labour government to allow country houses to be built in contravention of normal rural planning guidelines. This policy stated that such houses had to be sustainable and of exceptional architectural merit. Unfortunately, the planning inspector did not accept the arguments that Barry's house was of such merit, despite its accepted innovative and sustainable char-

acteristics; however, other natural builders may try to use this argument again in the future.

The Brithdir Mawr Battle

Another famous planning battle has been raging in the Pembrokeshire Coast National Park, where Tony Wrench and others built a low-impact round house without planning permission. For a while no one was aware of nor objected to the development. Legend has it that the project was spotted from the air because of sunlight reflected from a solar panel and thus the planning authority sprang into action. After several years' struggle, which included demonstrations to prevent a forced demolition, the project attracted international interest as well as support from establishment figures in Wales. Brithdir Mawr was granted some sort of reprieve as the National Park Authority decided not to proceed with an injunction to force demolition in the summer of 2005 until they had drawn up a new policy on low-impact developments.

TREADING LIGHTLY ON THE LAND

Going ahead and building without planning permission in an area such as a national park is not an approach that many would support. There is always the danger of creating a precedent for others who would carry out development that would not respect

178

the low-impact principles of Tony Wrench and like-minded others. On the other hand, their actions have prompted the planning authorities to draw up policies on low-impact developments which may make it possible for other, carefully controlled projects to be permitted in the future.

There is a world of difference between such a small, self-sufficient scheme, using a small area of land efficiently with natural building techniques, and a proposed holiday and leisure development on the edge of Pembrokeshire National Park costing £50 million with some 340 timber chalets surrounding a 'celtic village'. The irony of allowing such a massive development to go ahead when Brithdir Mawr still has an uncertain future is plain to many.

In other areas of rural England huge encampments of mobile homes have been established by farmers, without planning permission, to accommodate migrant workers to harvest crops and pick fruit. Along with acres of poly-tunnels, such unsustainable development is frequently justified on the basis of contributing to the local economy and creating jobs.

There are many people who want to live on the land and grow their own vegetables and keep their own chickens or manage local woodland but in a less dramatic fashion. These are not people with second homes but families committed to developing an alternative, more sustainable life style. Natural building techniques appeal to them and it is inevitable that planning policies will have to change to permit and facilitate such development. This movement has been well documented by Simon Fairlie and the Chapter 7 group who have been campaigning for some years to change planning policies to help people living on smallholdings and to carry out responsible low-impact projects in the countryside. Chapter 7 have published a collection of fascinating case studies of people with smallholdings who have gone back to the land to create a sustainable form of living. These pioneers all follow the principle that they should 'tread lightly on the land', but this is yet to be enshrined in British or Irish planning law.

These ideas have been put into practice in a number of low-impact settlements such as Tinkers Bubble in Somerset. The most celebrated example of this is Ben Law, whose Woodland House has featured on the television programme 'Grand Designs' and appears as an example in this book. Law was working to manage small woodlands and it was essential for him to be on the land to carry out this task. He has managed to gain planning permission for his natural built house, but the permission applied only to him and his family.

A report prepared for the Pembrokeshire Coast National Park Authority by Baker Associates makes fascinating reading because it attempts to describe the nature of what is referred to as Low Impact Development (LID) and how LID developments could be allowed in areas where planning permission might not normally be granted. The seriousness of these issues should be considered at a national level so that there is a positive, nationwide initiative to support those who wish to settle in the countryside and live in a sustainable way. To have natural building methods defined within the scope of planning policy would be a big step forward and the Pembrokeshire

Roundhouse entrance at Tinkers Bubble in Somerset, where a low-impact settlement in a forest has been allowed to remain for some years.

Overview of the eco-village development at The Wintles in Shropshire.

report is useful in this respect. However, it does seem strange that building in a low-impact way should be regarded as an exception to the norm.

ECO-VILLAGES AND SUSTAINABLE HOUSING DEVELOPMENTS

While there are individuals carrying out natural building developments in the countryside, there are also groups trying to establish eco-villages and other cooperative schemes where they can adopt a more sustainable life style. These projects are either initiated by developers such as BEDZED, in the London Borough of Sutton, which was initiated by the Peabody Housing Trust and Bio-Regional Ltd, or The Wintles in Bishops Castle, Shropshire, being built by a company established by Bob Tomlinson. A co-housing scheme has also been built in Stroud, which allows people to live as a community and share some facilities. All of these schemes exhibit some environmentally-friendly features, but, as they were dependent on selling houses into the market, the developers have been cautious in their adoption of natural building technologies.

In Ireland 'The Village' is being developed in Cloughjordan in County Tipperary and will have 130 houses, shops, small businesses and community facilities based on ecological principles when it has been completed. Some of the houses may exhibit natural building characteristics. A small eco-village in County Cork – The Hollies – pioneered the idea of sustainable building guidelines that were published in vol. 2 of *The Green Building Handbook*. The Hollies developers were unable to get planning permission for the number of houses that were planned, but a number of low-impact building experiments have been carried out there, including the construction of a large cob house. The Hollies has also run a number of successful courses on natural building methods. Eco-villages are not just being planned for the countryside, there are also proposals for similar concepts in cities such as Manchester and Bristol.

COMMUNITY LAND TRUSTS

Having established the concept of alternative settlements, not only will planning policies have to

change to take note of the growing demand for this way of living but new models of land ownership will also be required. Most eco-villages seem to involve people moving into an area to create an alternative way of living, but there are also many examples of local communities trying to take charge of the development in their area. There are a number of initiatives to establish community land trusts that will allow local people to both carry out and control local development. The most famous of these is on the island of Gigha in Scotland, where the local community were able to buy the land from their absentee landlord. They have introduced their own wind turbine scheme and many other projects. Proposals for community land trusts can be found throughout the United Kingdom, from Devon and the south-west to Wales and the north of England. As these projects adopt progressive, sustainable building principles, there will be opportunities for natural building methods to be used. Natural building may involve some difficult negotiations with the authorities at the moment, but it will become an essential part of new policies in the future.

Quite a number of local planning authorities have adopted sustainable building policy guidelines for developers and applicants and, while planning law does not necessarily back these up, they are serving to educate the public about the need to embrace environmental principles. Environmental organizations such as WWF and Bioregional have proposed the concept of one planet living. According to ecological footprint theories, we currently require the equivalent of 3.5 planets to sustain our life style and so to get down to one planet means a much simpler resource-efficient model. A number of proposed progressive developments are trying to work towards this concept such as 'Z-Squared' in the Thames Gateway (2,000 homes), whereas other model projects, such as the Greenwich Millennium Village or Dunham Massey on National Trust land in rural Cheshire, have fallen well short of it, using up natural habitats and significant levels of resources. There is a long way to go before the real demands of sustainability are recognized, but the experience of the pioneers of natural building will be invaluable.

CHAPTER 11

The Principles of Green Building

INTRODUCTION

This chapter is a somewhat polemical statement about the nature of green and natural building because it is important to address the political climate – in which natural builders have to operate. Natural builders are pioneers in a hostile land it is necessary to understand the context in which natural building is developing.

The construction industry is a powerful part of the economy of most countries, although in developing countries many people still rely on local materials. However, even when people are building with mud walls they will use galvanized products, which require quarrying, manufacturing and transportation. In wealthy countries architects, developers and builders believe that they can use whatever materials they fancy from any part of the world, and the materials supply industry is increasingly dominated by a small number of multinational companies with a global control of the market.

The supply and specification of materials is at the heart of green building. Buildings should always be designed to be energy-efficient, but to ensure that the building is not depleting non-renewable resources, is not polluting the planet nor damaging our health depends on being able to get the necessary materials to construct the building ethically and so that it is environmentally benign.

The main principles of green building are:

- to make buildings as energy-efficient as possible to minimize the use of fossil fuel
- to design the building to act passively, absorbing energy from the sun, ventilating naturally and

allowing the insulated fabric and thermal mass to work effectively
- to put the building on the site in a way that acts in harmony with the landscape and setting and minimizes disruption to the ecosystem
- to take responsibility for all the upstream and downstream impacts of decisions
- to minimize water usage and waste
- to select building materials and methods that are low energy and minimize resource depletion
- to avoid the use of material and methods that cause pollution
- to select materials that do not damage the health of manufacturing workers, building workers, building occupants and wildlife.

These principles are fairly straightforward but hard to adhere to unless you use natural, renewable materials. However, the vast majority of building projects address only some of these principles. Most architects and clients seem happy to cherry-pick these topics and use them when it is convenient. Even many buildings that are claimed to be green or that win green awards usually address only some of them. To deal with all of them means working *holistically*, an awkward word that simply means addressing all of them at the same time. In general, the technology and knowledge required to address all of these precepts is simple: it is 90 per cent commitment and 10 per cent expertise. It is the commitment that is missing in so many projects because it is easier just to opt for conventional solutions and standard practices.

Thus green and natural building is about making a commitment to follow all the principles as far as possible. Of course, compromises may inevitably be made. Sometimes doing many innovative things all at once can become overly complicated and a further principle of green building should be 'keep it simple'. Unfortunately, there are some professionals and officials who are keen to make this relatively simple process into something complicated and difficult to understand. These 'envirocrats' are men and women in business suits who have spotted a career opportunity in creating a bureaucracy of rules, systems and standards, which try to define how to be environmentally responsible. Most of them operate under the banner of 'sustainability' since this has become the most useful and officially acceptable term for green policies; but beware whenever you see the word sustainable, behind it lurks greenwash, an attempt to dress up business as usual as being environmentally acceptable.

ENVIRONMENTAL ASSESSMENT TOOLS

There are very many environmental assessment tools, guidelines, standards and checklists. Every local authority and development agency, government department and non-governmental organization has one or is developing one. Even though we all live on the same planet, are equally wasteful of resources and producing carbon emissions, each of these tools, guidelines and checklists is different. It is necessary to ask whether this environmental and academic cottage industry is doing much to improve the environmental performance of the building industry. There are dangers that it is successfully obfuscating the issues and making everyone very confused as to what he or she should actually be doing. The names of a handful of environmental assessment tools are given below:

- BREEAM
- CEEQUAL
- ECOHOME
- PAPOOSE
- SBAT
- GBTOOL
- SIGMA
- EASYECO
- LEED

- ATHENA
- TQ
- BSLCA
- ECO EFFECT
- ENVEST
- ECOTECT.

Architects and builders or self-builders using natural materials may ask what this has got to do with them. If they are using local clay and straw and second-hand materials with almost nothing manufactured or imported from a non-renewable resource, they know that they are creating a low-impact, environmentally friendly building and need no codes or assessment tools to tell them so.

However, the forest of environmental assessment tools and standards are necessary because mainstream industry will not do anything to address the environmental agenda unless they are persuaded to do so by a variety of voluntary codes or are forced to do so by legislation. Otherwise they will simply carry on as though the oil is not going to run out, global warming is a myth and pollution is a problem for someone else to deal with in the next century. In order to get mainstream industry to change its ways, many are campaigning for greater regulation. This will lead to many more new rules and codes that will impact on natural building techniques.

Some aspects of this may be helpful to natural building. If there are useful codes of practice and guidelines that say how to use materials and building systems properly, this will be of great benefit. But if natural materials and methods are not included in the many tick-box systems that are being devised, then they may get excluded from use, particularly in public sector projects. It will not matter how green or low-impact a method is, if there is no assessment attached to it, then it may be difficult to specify it.

GOVERNMENT POLICY

The British government commissioned a report in 2003 from a sustainable construction task group chaired by Sir John Harman and this has led to several initiatives towards a sustainable building code. New legislation was passed in 2004, the Secure and Sustainable Building Act, which enables Parliament to introduce sustainability requirements into the building regulations. Up to now the regulations have been concerned with health and safety and energy efficiency, but not sustainability or environmental performance. All of these initiatives are to be welcomed, but unfortunately government policy has not got to grips with the issues in sustainable construction. The Parliamentary Audit Committee has severely criticized policies stating that, 'The Government's housing policy is an alarming example of disjointed thinking ... the principal beneficiary of housing growth will be property developers, with the environment, we all depend upon, being the principal loser.' Their report went on to criticize the composition of the sustainable building code steering group, making the obvious point that it did not contain experts on sustainable construction:

There is ample representation from industry, Government and social housing groups on the Steering Group. Having being told in evidence that organisations such as BRE and the Energy Savings Trust would be invited on to the Group, we were surprised to see that there is no representation from any organisations that are directly involved in how to improve the environmental performance of buildings. It is incredible that the Government has not thought it important to have any representation from the organisations that have the greatest expertise in this area. This omission does not inspire us with confidence that the Code will result in significant and meaningful improvements in how houses are built or how their impacts on the environment are minimised.

THE LACK OF UNIVERSAL ENVIRONMENTAL STANDARDS

Currently, most environmental assessment tools are designed to generate income for the organizations that promote them. To use the tools means paying thousands of pounds for access to the software or system. To get an eco-assessment rating or eco-label requires substantial investment and the payment of fees that can only be afforded by large companies. The working groups concerned with developing

these tools also include representation from the major trade associations for materials such as cement and concrete, plastics and fossil-fuel-based insulation. However, despite the proliferation of standards, life-cycle analyses, environmental policy statements, there is no universal standard to which products can be compared.

Many companies which produce products that are relatively environmentally friendly, find themselves in a similar position to self-builders and small companies promoting natural building materials and methods. Because there are no clearly agreed standards by which the environmental performance of building materials can be assessed but a plethora of confusing assessment systems, almost anyone can call his products green and get away with it. Challenges through the advertising standards legislation might be a way of exposing some bogus claims, but at the moment it is a complete free-for-all. This makes it difficult for competitors who are doing their best to make environmentally responsible products to distinguish themselves in the marketplace. Often such companies refuse to take part in some of the green labelling schemes because they feel that the schemes are so discredited.

In a pilot study funded by the Engineering and Physical Sciences Research Council (EPSRC), the work of six companies, who were trying to manufacture and/or distribute green products, was examined. They faced several problems, but in particular the lack of national standards which would certify environmentally friendly products and distinguish them from the conventional. A second problem was that of the poor perception that eco-products would not be as good. They were all preoccupied with the need to break out of the 'green ghetto' and into the mainstream so that their output would increase and their products benefit from economies of scale.

ACCREDITING GREEN PRODUCTS

The Soil Association certifies organic food and the Forest Stewardship Council certifies responsibly grown timber, but the FSC logo is not as well known as the Soil Association's. Attempts to introduce Eco labels by the European Union have had little impact, although much of the scientific work that has gone on as part of Eco labelling is very important. The EU Construction Products Directive was agreed in 1988 and was meant to include environmental criteria, but while today you can buy a bag of cement with a CE mark on it, the CE mark is telling you little more than that this is a properly manufactured bag of cement.

The government is supporting very little work into the actual science of natural or energy-efficient building methods or supporting the development of real low-impact alternatives. There is still a great deal of scientific work to be done to explain the health and pollution impacts of conventional materials and how natural materials are so much better. If society knew the truth about the damage caused by products such as plastics, fire retardants and cement they would not be so careless in their use.

But green building should not mean a blanket ban on the use of materials such as concrete and plastics. Instead, they should be used in a careful and limited way when there are no low-impact, natural alternatives available. Sadly, at present materials are used carelessly and freely with little thought for the damage they might do. There will be absolutists who will never use cement or PVC, but most natural builders are pragmatists and accept that, used responsibly, polystyrene insulation, concrete foundations and synthetic plastic roofing membranes may have to be used as there are currently no alternatives readily available. Glass, for instance, is a relatively high embodied-energy product, but it would be hard to design a passive solar building without it.

RATING RECYCLED MATERIALS

In particular, there will be a difficult balancing act when we consider the use of second-hand materials. Recycling should be an essential part of green building in which we endeavour to reduce the use of non-renewable resources and recognize the vital part that waste and second-hand materials have to play. It is especially important to reuse environmentally un-friendly materials because, if they end up in landfill or are incinerated, they release toxic chemicals into the ground, water or air. If we can encapsulate them safely in our buildings then we are benefiting the planet as much as by using natural and renewable materials.

Cement can be made from fly ash recovered from power station waste. For the foreseeable future we shall continue to burn carbon-based materials for power and it is important that the waste material is used. Fly ash can produce better concrete than Portland cement. Reducing the production of Portland cement has to be one of the aims of the green building movement because of its high carbon emissions. It is also important to remember that to use alternatives to cement such as lime does not reduce the carbon burden significantly. Depending on the efficiency of production, lime will have 50–80 per cent of the embodied energy of cement. It is important to be honest about the differences between materials and not simply get into black and white condemnations.

OPENNESS ABOUT IMPACTS

More openness and honesty in the building materials trade would make everyone's job much easier. However, our laws do not require manufacturers to declare the full constituents of their products, how much energy has been used in their manufacture and whether there are any pollution burdens. These issues are regarded as commercially sensitive, and even the manufacturers of environmentally benign products remain secretive in fear that their competitors will steal their formulae. This makes it difficult for the natural builder to be sure of what he is using if manufacturing is involved.

Some green statements about products are simply silly. Envirocrats carry out environmental audits or studies that are then selectively quoted in the promotional literature. Both the Copper and the Zinc Development Association point out that we need zinc and copper in our diets to keep us healthy, as though this is somehow related to the use of the materials in building. Copper and zinc are both environmentally reasonable options, in fact, because of the amounts that are recycled, but it is not easy to get accurate figures on how much comes from recycled stock and how much from virgin mining.

As there are so many environmental rating systems it is difficult to decide which one to rely on. All use different criteria and weightings, some will give greater weight to life-cycle analysis, performance in use or ultimate disposal, others will give greater weight to embodied energy or their ability to reduce energy consumption, and yet others will weight resource depletion higher. Unfortunately, to the uninformed it may appear that certain standards are absolute and authorized by the government, whereas in practice they are mostly paid for by the companies that are selling the materials. Instead of there being global agreement over some baseline standards, every country has a different approach with Australia, the USA, Germany and Scandinavia having some of the more open systems.

RATING PRODUCTS

One of the leading British standards is that provided by the BRE (which is no longer a government body, but owned by a private trust). An example of the use of their environmental profiling methodology can be found in an advertising brochure for a vinyl-flooring product:

> We can now report that two of our products, 'XYZ' standard XL 2mm sheet vinyl and 'ZYX' PUR 2mm sheet vinyl, are now certified through BRE Certification Ltd for their environmental profiles. When the 'Eco-points' measured and reported in this certification are compared to BRE's Green Guide to Specification, the products achieve the highest possible rating 'A', over a sixty-year life. The BRE method of environmental profiling ensures that reliable and comparable environmental information is available between competing products, thus eliminating the confusion of claims and counterclaims about the performance of building materials.

Giving an 'A' rating to vinyl flooring is unlikely to eliminate confusion, since very few natural builders would be willing to use a vinyl product, which in this case is also polyurethane-coated. Natural builders would be applying different criteria since they would consider fossil-fuel usage and the chemicals involved in vinyl production. They might choose linoleum, tiles, wood or earth on their floor, but such a choice would not necessarily be underwritten by the BRE's highly influential 'Eco points' system, which is also used in the government-approved 'Eco-Homes'

standard. Thus the enthusiastic green builder has to wade through a swamp of contradictory information, confusing and often impenetrable assessment systems and technical data. Taking personal responsibility for the environmental impact of a mud building in your back garden is relatively easy, but, if you are doing a project for a local authority or a business with complicated procurement and tendering rules, environmental policy statements may be mandatory.

What is most important is that proponents of natural building have to engage with the mainstream and find a way to cope with the complexities of the commercial and bureaucratic world we inhabit. Avoiding building and planning regulations and standards is not the answer, instead we need vigorous and strong natural building trade associations and lobbying groups that will campaign to ensure that we are not saddled with narrow standards and tick-box systems which ignore low-impact building.

GENERIC AGRÉMENT CERTIFICATES?

One interesting model in South Africa is the concept of generic 'agrément' certificates for alternative materials. Most commercially available materials and products go to the British (or Irish) Board of Agrément and submit all their technical information for checking. The BBA then validates this work and issue a certificate that is generally accepted in the industry that a material is fit for purpose and often required as part of specifications and insurance schemes. The Agrément certificates are paid for by the manufacturers and are tied to the particular product. However, work has been done in South Africa to produce a generic certificate for earth construction, not tied to a particular product but which sets standards and best practice for a material in general and is freely available for all to use. This would seem to be a way forward for the natural building movement, if sufficient funds can be raised to pay for the testing and validation. Unfortunately at the moment, the system is geared to the development of patented products and materials and thus knowledge and expertise is privatized. This is even extending into the natural building sector with patented earth, lime, paint and hemp products, for example.

DEVELOPING THE SCIENCE

Much of the building science currently applied to construction materials and methods is not appropriate to natural building. The measurement of structural integrity, insulation standards and performance is defined by the pragmatic needs of the industry rather than pure physics and chemistry. Because of this, natural material and building methods can appear to function less successfully than synthetic mainstream products. In order to challenge this it will be necessary to go back to the science of materials and buildings and even to rewrite some of the textbooks. This process has begun, but it is difficult for academic engineers and scientists to get government research funding for this sort of work. Many of the bodies and officials responsible for awarding research grants are influenced by mainstream industrial vested interests, which are even represented on awards committees. Where research proposals are 'peer-reviewed' they often go out to people who are being funded by private industry. Trade associations are well represented on scientific committees that determine standards and regulations and often exert an undue influence. Much of the intellectual knowledge about the science of materials is locked up in private companies and they are rarely willing to share this with the wider community.

But some positive changes can be seen. The British government has established the National Non Food Crops Centre in York, which is concerned with the promotion of crop-based, renewable products. However, its funding is tiny compared with that given by the government to subsidize non-sustainable alternatives. The British Department of Trade and Industry has supported some research on earth building and sustainable masonry research has been supported by the EPSRC. However, the funding is often directed at the promotion of technology or applications in industry when what is really needed is support for the underpinning science. Natural building possibilities are not glamorous and high-tech, rarely involve computer technology or 'intelligent systems' and are hard to patent and thus create investment opportunities for venture capitalists and merchant bankers. Indeed, many natural builders would be ideologically against the idea of sustainable technologies being privatized and used for the profits of large corporations.

On the other hand, it is necessary to find ways of getting materials adopted by mainstream industry. If natural building remains a quirky, marginalized activity, perceived as being only for hippies and drop-outs, then many of the excellent building techniques will not be taken up on a larger scale. Understanding the science of materials is the key to this. If we can demonstrate that natural materials perform better than fossil-fuel-based materials, both in terms of environmental impact, buildability, robustness and life-cycle performance, then we can ensure a greater take-up. Challenging the bogus claims of greenwash-type environmental profiles will be crucial, but it can only be done if it is backed up by solid science. This is an enormous challenge.

Bibliography

CHAPTER 1

Alexander, C., *The Timeless Way of Building* (Oxford University Press, Oxford, 1979)

Association of Environment Conscious Builders (www.aecb.net)

Brand, S., *How Buildings Learn: What happens after They're Built* (Viking, London, 1994)

Elizabeth, L. and Adams, C., *Alternative Construction – Contemporary Natural Building Methods* (Wiley, New York, 2000)

May, N., *Breathability*, unpublished paper (www.natural-buildings.co.uk)

Rudofsky, B., *Architecture without Architects: A Short Introduction to Non-pedigreed Architecture* (University of New Mexico, 1972)

CHAPTER 2

Elizabeth, L. and Adams, C. op cit., *Alternative Construction – Contemporary Natural Building Methods* (Wiley, New York, 2000)

Houben, H. and Guillaud, H., *Earth Construction: A Comprehensive Guide* (Intermediate Technology Publications, London, 1994)

Kennedy, J. *et al.*, *The Art of Natural Building; Design; Construction, Resources* (New Society Publishers, Gabriola Island, British Columbia, Canada, 2002)

King, B., *Buildings of Earth and Straw* (Ecological Design Press, Sausalito, CA, 1996)

Little, R. and Morton, T., *Building with Earth in Scotland: Innovative Design and Sustainability* (Scottish Executive Central Research Unit, Edinburgh, 2001)

McCann, J., *Clay and Cob Buildings* (Shire Books, Princes Risborough, 2004)

Minke, G., *Earth Construction Handbook: The Building Material Earth in Modern Architecture* (WIT Press, Southampton, 2000)

Morton, T. *et al.*, *Low Cost Earth Brick Construction at 2 Kirk Park Dalguise – Monitoring and Evaluation* (Arc Architects, Auchtermuchty, 2005; www.arc-architects.co.uk)

Norton, J., *Building with Earth: A Handbook* (Intermediate Technology Publications, London, 1997)

O'Neill County Historical Society, *A Study of Mud-Wall Building in the Blackwater Basin* (Bantry, 2001)

Schofield, J. and Smallcombe, J., *Cob Buildings: A Practical Guide* (Black Dog Press, Crediton, 2004; www.abeysmallcombe.com)

Walker, P. *et al.*, *Rammed Earth Design and Construction Guidelines* (BRE Bookshop, Watford, 2005)

Williams Ellis, C., Eastwick Field, J. and E., *Building in Cob Pisé and Stabilised Earth* (Country Life, London, 1919)

CHAPTER 3

Aaron, J.R. and Richards, E.G., *British Woodland Produce* (Stobart Davies, London, 1990)

Abbott, M., *Green Woodwork – Working with Wood the Natural Way* (Guild of Master Craftsmen, Lewes, 1989)

Border Oak, Kingsland, Leominster, Herefordshire (www.borderoak.com)

Borer, P. and Harris, C., *Out of the Woods – Ecological Designs for Timber Frame Housing* (CAT Publications, Machynlleth, 1998)

Edminster, A. (ed.), *Building with Vision – Optimising and Finding Alternatives to Wood* (Watershed Media, Healdsburg, CA, 2001)

Evans, B., 'In the Frame', *Architects Journal* (15 July 2004).

Forest Stewardship Council, UK Working Group, Room 8, 11–13 Great Oak Street, Llanidloes, Powys, SY18 6BU (www.fsc-uk.org)

Janssen, J.J.A., *Building with Bamboo – A Handbook* (Intermediate Technology Development Group, London, 1995)

Kindersley Centre, Sheepdrove Organic Farm, Lambourn, Berks, RG17 7UU (www.sheepdrove.com)

Law, B., *The Woodland Way – A Permaculture Approach to Sustainable Woodland Management* (Permanent Publications, East Meon, 2001)

Law, B., *The Woodland House* (Permanent Publications, East Meon, 2005) (www.permaculture.co.uk)

Segal Self Build Trust (www.segal-selfbuild.co.uk)

The Wintles (www.livingvillage.com)

Thompson, C., *Window of Opportunity – The Environmental and Economic Benefits of Specifying Timber Window Frames* (WWF-UK, Godalming, 2005)

Vitra Design Museum, *Grow Your Own House – Simon Velez and Bamboo Architecture* (Vitra Design Museum, Weil Am Rhein, 2000)

Warren, A., 'The Crucks of the Matter', *Building for a Future* 03/05, Green Building Press (www.newbuilder.co.uk)

Welsh Timber Forum (www.welshtimberforum.co.uk)

Wood for Good Campaign (www.woodforgood.com)

CHAPTER 4

Bergeron, M. and Lacinski, P., *Serious Straw Bale* (Chelsea Green Publishing, White River Junction, Vermont, USA, 2000)

Borer, P. and Harris, C., *The Whole House Book* (Centre for Alternative Technology, Machynlleth, 1998)

Elizabeth, L. and Adams, C. (eds), *Alternative Construction, Contemporary Natural Building Methods* (Wiley, New York, 2000)

Goodhew, S., Griffiths, R. and Woolley, T., 'An Investigation of the Moisture Content in the Walls of a Straw-bale Building', *Building and Environment* (vol. 39, pp. 1443–51, 2004) (www.sciencedirect.com)

Gray, A. and Hall, A., *Straw Bale Homebuilding* (Earth Garden Books, Victoria, Australia, 2000)

Jones, B., *Building with Straw Bales* (Green Books, Totnes, 2002)

Kennedy, J., Smith, M. and Wanek, C. (eds) op cit., *The Art of Natural Building* (New Society Publishers, Gabriola Island, British Columbia, Canada, 2002)

King, B. op cit., *Buildings of Earth and Straw* (Ecological Design Press, Sausalito, CA, 1996)

McGregor, S. and Trulsson, N., *Living Homes, Sustainable Architecture and Design* (Chronicle Books, San Francisco, 2001)

MacDonald, S. and Myrhmann, M., *Build it with Bales* (Out on Bale, Tucson, AZ, 1998)

Phillipson, M., *Thermal and Moisture Performance of Strawbale Housing* (Client Report no. 16061, Building Research Establishment, East Kilbride, 2003)

Steen, A. and B., Bainbridge, D. and Eisenberg, D., *The Straw Bale House* (Chelsea Green Publishing, VT, 1994)

Steen, A. and B., *The Beauty of Straw Bale Homes* (Chelsea Green Publishing, VT, 2004)

The Ecological Building Network (www.ecobuildnetwork.org)

Wanek C., 'Straw Bale Building: Lessons Learned', in Kennedy *et al.*, op.cit.

Woolley, T. and Kimmins, S., 'Straw Bale Building', in *Green Building Handbook*, Vol. 2, Ch. 9 (Spon, London, 2000)

CHAPTER 5

Crosby, R., 'BC's Shawood Lumber is finding a ready market for its FSC certified wood in environmentally friendly conscious Europe', *Logging and Sawmilling Journal* (October, 2004) (www.forestnet.com)

Green Roofs for Architects, *Architects' Journal Conference Pack* (15 June 2005)

Law, B. op cit., *The Woodland House* (Permanent Publications, East Meon, 2005)

Nash, R., *Thatchers and Thatching* (Batsford, London, 1991), Thatching UK (www.thatch.org)

West, N., *Thatch: A Manual for Owners, Surveyors Architects and Builders* (David & Charles, Newton Abbot, 1987)

Williams, A., 'Hines suggested that green roofs need no maintenance at all – including watering', *Architects' Journal* (7 July 2005, pp. 38–41)

CHAPTER 6

Allen, G. *et al.*, *Hydraulic Lime Mortar for Stone, Brick and Block Masonry* (Donhead Publishing, Shaftesbury, 2003)

Calch Ty-Mawr Lime: The Welsh Centre for Traditional and Ecological Building (www.tymawrlime.org.uk)

Holmes, S. and Wingate, M., *Building with Lime: A Practical Introduction* (Intermediate Technology Publications, London, 1997)

King, B., *Making Better Concrete – Guidelines for Using Fly Ash for Higher Quality Eco-Friendly Structures* (Green Building Press, San Rafael, California, 2005)

Limetec/IJP Lime (www.limetechnology.co.uk)

Pritchett, I., 'Energy Masonry', in Roaf, S. *et al.* (eds), *Eco-House 3* (Architectural Press, Elsevier, Oxford, 2006)

St Astier Lime (www.stastier.co.uk)

UK Building Limes Forum (www.buildinglimesforum.org.uk)

Wingate, M., *Small-scale Lime-burning* (Intermediate Technology Publications, London, 1985)

CHAPTER 7

Construire en Chanvre (French Hemp Construction Association), BP 6, F-89150 Saint-Valerien, France (www.construction-chanvre.asso.fr)

Cripps, A., *Crops in Construction* (Construction Industry Research and Information Association, RP680, London, 2004) (www.lhoist.com)

ENTPE (École Nationale de Travaux Public l'État); Dr Laurent Arnaud, Départment Genie Civil et Bâtiment, Rue Mauric Audin, 69518 Vaulx-en-Velin, France

Evrard, A. (ed.), *Betons de Chanvre, Synthese des proprietes physiques* (Construire en Chanvre, Saint-Valerien, France, November 2002)

Suffolk Housing Society, *Homes from Hemp*, A Building Technique for the Future, Summary Research Findings (Bury St Edmunds, 2002)

UK Hemp Lime Construction Products Association, PO Box 101, Buxton, Derbyshire SK17 0WT (www.hemplime.org.uk)

Yates, T. (ed.), *Final Report on the Construction of the Hemp Houses at Haverhill, Suffolk* (Client Report No.209 717 rev1, Building Research Establishment, Watford, October 2002)

CHAPTER 8

Construction Resources, *Product Information Catalogue: Products and Systems for Sustainable Building* (Great Guildford Street, London SE1 0HS, 2004) (www.constructionresources.com)

Cripps, A. *et al.*, *Crops in Construction Handbook* (CIRIA, London, C614, November 2004 (www.ciria.org)

Green Building Store, *Natural Insulation* (www.ecoproducts.co.uk/ins, 2005)

Impetus Consulting, *Market Review of Renewable Insulation Materials – A Summary* (London, March 2002) (www.impetusconsult.co.uk)

May, N., *Breathability* (unpublished paper, 2005, available through www.natural-building.co.uk)

Natural Building Technologies, Insulation leaflet (Worminghall, Bucks., www.natural-building.co.uk)

Szokolay, S.V., *Introduction to Architectural Science – The Basis of Sustainable Design* (Architectural Press, Oxford, 2004)

Van Dam, J.W.E., 'Product Development from Renewable Resources – Agro food chain entering construction markets', *Sustainable Building* No.01 (Aeneas Technical Publishers, Netherlands, 2005)

CHAPTER 9

Construction Resources, *Product Information Products and Systems for Sustainable Building* (Great Guildford Street, London SE1 0HS, 2005) (www.constructionresources.com)

Edwards, L. and Lawless, J., *The Natural Paint Book: The Complete Guide to Natural Paints, Recipes and Finishes* (Kyle Cathie, London, 2002)

Green Building Store (www.greenbuildingstore.co.uk)

Guelberth, C.R. and Chiras, D., *The Natural Plaster Book* (New Society Publishers, Gabriola Island, British Columbia, Canada, 2003)

Hawkes, N., 'Household Chemicals in Direct Link to Asthma Rise', *The Times* (23 December 2004)

Howieson, S., *Housing and Asthma* (Spon Press, Abingdon, 2005)

MacRae, F., 'Poisoned in the womb' (*Daily Mail*, 8 September 2005)

May, N., *Paints and Ecology* (Natural Building Technologies, Worminghall Road, Oakley, Bucks.) (www.naturalbuildings.co.uk, 2005)

Mike Wye & Associates, Buckland Filleigh, Beaworthy, Devon (www.mikewye.co.uk)

The Green Shop Paint Catalogue (Stroud, www.greenshop.co.uk)

Thomas, P., *Living Dangerously: Are Everyday Toxins Making You Sick?* (Gill & Macmillan, Dublin, 2003)

Traditional Lime Co., Rath, Tullow, County Carlow, Ireland (www.traditionallime.com)

Ty-Mawr Lime Ltd, Llangasty, Brecon, Powys (www.lime.org.uk)

Woolley, T. and Kimmins, S., *The Green Building Handbook* (Spon Press, Abingdon, Vol.1, 1997, Vol. 2, 2000)

WWF-UK, *Contamination: The Results of WWF'S Biomonitoring Survey* (Godalming, 2003, www.wwf.org.uk)

CHAPTER 10

Baker Associates, *Low Impact Development Further Research Final Report* (Pembrokeshire Coast National Park Authority, 2004)

Chapter 7 and the PPG 7 Reform Group, *Sustainable Homes and Livelihoods in the Countryside* (Chapter 7, South Petherton, Somerset, www.thelandisours.org)

Cornwall Sustainable Building Trust (www.csbt.org.uk)

Fairlie, S., 'Low Impact Development' (Jon Carpenter Publishing, Chipping Norton, 1997)

Fairlie, S. and the TLIO Rural Planning Group, 'Defining Rural Sustainability, Consultation Paper on Low-impact Rural Development' (S. Fairlie, Tinker's Bubble, Stoke-sub-Hamdon, Somerset TA14 6TE) (www.thelandisours.org)

'Good News for the Roundhouse at Brithdir Mawr', *Permaculture Magazine* (No. 45) (information on the Wrench roundhouse, www.thatroundhouse.info)

Somerset Trust for Sustainable Development (www.sustainablehousing.org.uk)

The Bluestone Development (www.cprw.org.uk/margatel/bluestone)

Wackernagel, M. and Rees, W., *Our Ecological Footprint* (New Society Publishers, Gabriola Island, British Columbia, 1996)

Wrench, T., *Building a Low Impact Roundhouse*, A Simple Living Series Book (Permanent Publications, East Meon, 2000)

CHAPTER 11

Fox, W. (ed.), *Ethics and the Built Environment* (Routledge, London, 2002)

Harman, J. and Benjamin, V., *Better Buildings, Better Lives – Report of the Sustainable Building Task Group*, www.odpm.gov.uk (May 2004)

House of Commons Environmental Audit Committee, *Housing: Building a Sustainable Future* (House of Commons Paper 135-I, 135-II, 2004)

King, B., *Making Better Concrete – Guidelines to Using Fly Ash for Higher Quality Eco-Friendly Structures* (Green Building Press, San Rafael, 2005)

Woolley, T., 'Balanced Value – a Review and Critique of Sustainability Assessment Methods', in Yang, J. *et al.*, *Smart and Sustainable Built Environments* (Blackwell, Oxford, 2005)

Woolley, T. and Caleyron, N., 'Overcoming the barriers to the greater development and use of environmentally friendly construction materials' (Sustainable Building International Conference Proceedings, Oslo, 2002)